Economics and Politics
of Industrial Policy

MONOGRAPHS IN COMPARATIVE PUBLIC POLICY

Werner J. Feld, General Editor

About the Book and Editors

Industrial policy is a good example of the growing economic and political interdependency between Europe and the United States. The contributors to this volume, which compiles the proceedings of the seventh conference sponsored by the Institute for the Comparative Study of Public Policy, examine the ways in which national, and supranational in the case of the European Community, industrial policies are implemented. It is thought that diversity within the country is the primary reason why the United States does not have a comprehensive national policy. There is a consensus among the authors that the U.S. economy is less subject or amenable to central government planning than the economies of Europe. In Europe, there is more interest in coordinating industrial policy throughout the European Community, but here too the failure to adopt a comprehensive policy reveals the enormous diversity and parochialism that conflict with supranational goals. The contributors conclude that while a centrally planned and implemented industrial policy may be desirable, we do not have the means to achieve it. Acknowledging the major industrial and trade problems facing the United States and Western Europe, the authors feel that it is not clear whether these problems can be resolved by government intervention.

Steven A. Shull is professor of political science at the University of New Orleans. Jeffrey E. Cohen is associate professor of political science at the same institution.

Published in cooperation
with the Institute for the
Comparative Study of Public Policy,
The University of New Orleans/
The University of Innsbruck

Economics and Politics
of Industrial Policy
The United States
and Western Europe

edited by Steven A. Shull
and Jeffrey E. Cohen

Westview Press / Boulder and London

Monographs in Comparative Public Policy

This Westview softcover edition was manufactured on our own premises using
equipment and methods that allow us to keep even specialized books in stock.
It is printed on acid-free paper and bound in softcovers that carry the
highest rating of the National Association of State Textbook Administrators,
in consultation with the Association of American Publishers and the Book
Manufacturers' Institute.

Copyright © 1986 by the Institute for the Comparative Study of Public Policy

Published in 1986 in the United States of America by Westview Press, Inc.;
Frederick A. Praeger, Publisher; 5500 Central Avenue, Boulder, Colorado 80301

Library of Congress Cataloging in Publication Data
Economics and politics of industrial policy.
   (Monographs in comparative public policy)
   Bibliography: p.
   1. Industry and state--United States--Addresses,
essays, lectures. 2. Industry and state--Europe--
Addresses, essays, lectures. I. Shull, Steven A.
II. Cohen, Jeffrey E. III. Series.
HD3616.U47E34   1986   338.94   85-26478
ISBN 0-8133-7140-6

Composition for this book was provided by the editors.
This book was produced without formal editing by the publisher.

Printed and bound in the United States of America

The paper used in this publication meets the requirements of the
American National Standard for Permanence of Paper for Printed
Library Materials Z39.48-1984.

10 9 8 7 6 5 4 3 2 1

Contents

Foreword

It is a distinct privilege that we present in this
volume the proceedings of the seventh annual symposium
organized jointly by the University of New Orleans and
the University of Innsbruck on February 21-22, 1985, in
New Orleans. "The Economics and Politics of Industrial
Policy" is of crucial importance for the economic development of the advanced Western nations as they face
each other and as they must cope with the gradual industrialization of the Third World. Since industrial and
labor conditions differ from country to country, comparative analyses of these conditions, especially in the
United States and Western Europe, are likely to offer
insights and issues that may be useful in determining
whether and how the initiation of specific policies can
provide remedies for countering harmful economic trends
in various nation-states and increase the quality of
life of their people. This complex of issues was addressed by five scholars during the symposium; their
presentations then became the topic for observations by
mostly local and regional leaders who brought their
practical experiences to bear on the questions of industrial policy.
     The main chapters of this volume contain the schol-
arly presentations made during the symposium. They are
authored by Dr. Robert Z. Lawrence of the Brookings Institution (keynote essay); Dr. Volkmar Lauber, University of Salzburg; Dr. B. Guy Peters, University of Pitts-
burgh; Drs. Jeffrey E. Cohen, University of New Orleans,
and Gregory G. Brunk, University of Oklahoma (co-authors);
and Dr. Anton Pelinka, University of Innsbruck. The
contributions of the panelists came from Ollie D. Brown,
a corporation president; William T. Hackett, Assistant
Secretary of Commerce, State of Louisiana; Carl Crowe,
a labor union official; Joan C. Felts, real estate executive; Joel C. Myers, League of Women Voters local president; and Dr. Toussaint Hocevar, University of New
Orleans professor of economics.

x

We would like to express our sincere appreciation for the high quality of all contributions and comments and thank the panel moderators for the managerial talents displayed.

Gordon H. Mueller, Dean
Metropolitan College
University of New Orleans

Werner J. Feld, Director
Institute for the Comparative
Study of Public Policy
University of New Orleans

Preface

The seventh biannual symposium organized by the University of New Orleans and the University of Innsbruck focused on a topic of interdisciplinary interest--industrial policy--analyzed by economists, political scientists, legal experts and others. The main speakers were chosen to bring together approaches typical for American and European scientists, and the academic results reflect the realities of both.

The publication of the symposium proceedings offers the broader academic community the opportunity to use the outcome of this international meeting and permits the use of this outcome by the business and political communities as well. The basic assumption is that everybody has to learn--Europeans and Americans, political scientists and economists--through academic research and social reality.

The University of New Orleans and the University of Innsbruck are linked not only by a formal friendship agreement, but also by a well established network of activities: exchange of students, faculty, and research. The interdisciplinary symposia and their publication are part of this. It is in the interest of both universities to promote new activities, e.g., a program for research planned and implemented by the two universities. The already established cooperation should be the challenge to develop even further levels of cooperation.

Anton Pelinka
Professor and Chairman of the
Department of Political Science, University of Innsbruck;
Coordinator for Cooperation
Between the Universities of
New Orleans and Innsbruck

1
Introduction

*Steven A. Shull**

Though the term "industrial policy" is a relatively recent addition to the vocabulary of scholars and policymakers, governments have had a long history of using
such policies. Part of the reason for the need for a
new term is that the economies of the major Western industrialized nations have undergone major changes in
recent years which have undermined the integrity of
their economies. Also important is the fact that economic problems and policies have been transformed from
discrete to interlocked problems. Some years ago,
Aaron Wildavsky (1966) wrote on the transformation of
foreign policy, arguing that domestic concerns have come
to be important to foreign policy decision makers. Where
domestic concerns meet foreign policy has been called
"intermestic policy" by Anderson and his colleagues
(1984). We see the same type of transformation in the
economic policy realm, as formerly discrete economic
problems and policy subsystems have turned into con-
nected problems within the economic macrosystem. Such
a transformation has also been noted in the environmen-
tal and energy policy areas (Anderson et al., 1984).
The use of the term "industrial policy" captures this
policy transformation in the economic policy realm.
    The breadth of industrial policy leads, however,
to some confusion over the precise meaning of the term.
Three broad types of economic policies can be subsumed
under this label (Olson, 1985). The first is macroeconomic policy, which involves the use of fiscal and
monetary instruments to affect the economy as a whole.
Second is international trade policy; and third are the
more specific policies aimed at particular industries
or economic sectors. For instance, import quotas, domestic content legislation, and manpower policies are
all varieties of this third type.

*I am grateful to Jeffrey E. Cohen, Lance T. LeLoup,
and Werner J. Feld for helpful comments on the Introduction and Conclusion and to Stephanie Rondenell for typ-
ing them and in helping to put together this symposium.

1

However, further confusing the definition of industrial policy is the fact that purpose governmental in-action may also be a government policy. Laissez-faire, the view that government should not interfere with the general economy, has been revived as theory and also as a policy option over the past decade. This is especially true in the United States and Great Britain. One difficulty of assessing industrial policy, then, is distinguishing between purposive governmental inaction and the government's inability to act.

Industrial policy does not fall neatly into any standard and recognized categories of public policies. The interlocking nature of various economic problems include policies with distributive as well as redistributive characteristics. Moreover, as we will see, the American and European reactions emphasize the distributive and redistributive qualities of industrial policy differently. Basically, American industrial policy leans more toward the distributive side, while European industrial policies have a stronger redistributive component.

Industrial policy is a broad, ambiguous concept that means different things to different people (Connerly, 1983; Olson, 1985). Economist Lester Thurow sees industrial policies as working in three different ways in advanced capitalist countries:

> A government agency is established to partially finance research and development on new products or new production processes....
>
> Government seeks systematically to reduce the costs of capital and increase its availability to industrial firms....
>
> The government has some systemic procedure...to see if it is workable and, if it is, what cooperative government actions are needed to complement those promised by industry and labor (Thurow, 1985, p. 29).

Thurow's formulation sounds straightforward, but industrial policy defies neat definition. Seemingly, it relates to government efforts to increase the influence of industry specifically. On a more general level, one can think of it as any government policy designed to promote or facilitate changes in the operation of the economy. Most industrial policies fall into one of two categories, roughly put, "picking winners" versus finding remedies for faltering industries.

Great Britain traditionally has used industrial policy to save declining heavy industry. The government infused money into many ailing industries and also nationalized to some degree the coal, steel, automobile, and shipbuilding industries. One critic suggests that such policies "seem to be devoted to creating an industrial museum" (Denzau, 1983, p. 3). However, defenders

note that Britain might have lost all domestic steel
and auto production without government assistance--a
situation completely unpalatable both politically and
strategically.

The United States has also backed failing industries, e.g., the Chrysler bailout in the late 1970s.
Facing bankruptcy and the loss of hundreds of thousands
of jobs, the government fashioned a loan and loan guarantee program to keep the giant corporation afloat.
Only a few years later, this third largest U.S. auto
manufacturer was able to pay off the loans early. Some
still dispute the success of the program, arguing that
Japan's voluntary import restrictions were the primary
reason for Chrysler's success. Still, one can point to
Chrysler as an important example of the success (even
if it proves temporary) of an industrial policy that
backs traditional companies in trouble. "Losers" can
turn into "winners" (Barker, 1984).

The strategy of picking winners is more controversial. Robert Reich proposes this strategy in his book,
The Next American Frontier (1983). The government, says
Reich, should establish policies to promote and foster
the new high-tech growth industries. The government
should attempt to redirect resources away from the traditional industries which are on the decline to new
fields such as computers, micro chips, aerospace, and
other coming areas. Japanese success is cited as support. The Japanese Ministry of International Trade and
Industry (MITI), according to some, separates winners
from losers and created a "miracle by design" (Johnson,
1982). Proponents suggest that an agency could be created in the United States to help foster economic growth,
productivity increases, and the transition of economic
resources from noncompetitive areas to new growth areas
(Eckstein et al., 1984; Presidential Commission, 1985;
Rohatyn, 1984).

An alternative view focuses on free trade and its
foundation, the theory of comparative advantage. The
open exchange of goods between nations allows each to
export what it produces most efficiently and cheaply
and to import those goods which other countries produce
more effectively. The net result is higher productivity, lower consumer prices, and generally greater growth.
So why do not all the nations of the world simply elim-
inate tariffs and other trade barriers? Because strong
domestic pressures for protection exist in virtually all
developed economies. Whether it is inefficient French
farmers, the British auto industry, or American steel,
domestic politics demand protection from competitive imports. Thus, industrial policy has to be considered in
all of its ramifications: economic, social, and political.

Although the meaning and definition of industrial
policy are unclear and subject to dispute, two concepts

should help to organize the views of our authors and
lead us to a greater understanding. The first concept,
policy context, refers to the structural and environ-
mental forces surrounding policymaking. Just a few
examples of these forces are political parties, interest
groups, and bureaucratic and constitutional forces. It
reminds us that many governmental and nongovernmental
actors influence the formulation and execution of public
policy. While this may be even more true in the United
States than in Europe, policy in all industrial democracies involves many conditions. The second concept to
enhance our understanding is policy content, which refers to the substance of policies themselves. Many
scholars argue that demarcating issues into familiar
policy categories (both substantive and functional typologies) not only allows for comparison but may even contribute to explaining the policymaking process. Perhaps
it is easier to identify roles of participants than to
categorize industrial policy precisely, but both concepts assist in describing, explaining, and, perhaps
even predicting the prospects for industrial policies
in America and Western Europe.

POLICY CONTEXT

The essays in this volume concern industrial policy
primarily in the world's most industrialized countries.
While Japan receives some attention because it has the
world's most extensive industrial policy, the primary
focus here is on Western Europe and the United States.
The contrasts are considerable since the American economy is less subject to central planning than in most
European countries. The inability or perhaps the dis-
inclination of the U.S. government to impose a centralized industrial policy does not preclude a vigorous
debate by both proponents and opponents of greater government intervention. Nevertheless, in the United
States, industrial policies have been widely discussed
(Dolbeare, 1984; Phillips, 1984; Reich, 1983; Rohatyn,
1984; Stein, 1983).
     How unique is the American situation in this? One
of the oldest public policies in American history concerns foreign trade: Should there be tariffs to protect
domestic industries, or is a free exchange of goods between nations more desirable? Trade is even more of an
issue today. Should there be a quota on the number of
Japanese cars imported? Should the United States restrict cheap shoes and textiles coming in from Korea,
Taiwan, and other countries? How much steel should be
imported from Europe? Does the strong dollar make it
too hard for U.S. companies to sell their products overseas?
     In its early years, the United States was primarily
a trading nation, a major supplier of raw materials,

agricultural goods, rum, and other such products.
Throughout the nineteenth century, Congress debated the
advisability of tariffs on imported manufactured goods
to protect fledgling American industries. The United
States continued to be a net importer of manufactured
goods and the recipient of foreign capital (Weidenbaum,
1983, pp. 34-35). By the beginning of this century,
however, the U.S. economy transformed. Trade accounted
for less and less of the GNP as the economic system became more self-sufficient. By 1960, exports .and imports
averaged only around 5 percent of gross national product.
     Beginning in 1960, foreign trade once again began
to increase relative to the size of the domestic economy.
By 1980, import and export transactions amounted to
around 12.5 percent of the GNP. Today, the United States
imports more goods than it exports, but exports more
services than it imports. Much of the trade deficit in
the United States in the 1970s and 1980s resulted from
dependence on foreign oil and the importation of Japanese goods, especially automobiles and electronic goods.
     Trade, like other economic policies, often is in
competition with other economic and political demands.
That many were unhappy with the number of imports in
the United States and the strength of the dollar abroad
reflects the continuing difficulty of coordinating and
balancing various economic policies in the United
States. Many writers, including our contributors, believe the diversity of the United States prevents a more
coordinated industrial policy.
     How does this American context of industrial policy
compare with what is occurring in Europe? First, Europe
is not a single entity--it is made up of different nations pursuing different industrial policies. In many
respects, the problems and prospects of developing comprehensive policies are quite similar on both sides of
the Atlantic. With the exception of recovery from
world wars, there has not been much support for government intervention in the economies of European nations
until recently, a situation which is similar to that in
the United States. The general feeling has been that
market forces were sufficient for economic development.
But market forces pitted the nations of Europe against
each other, and parochialism and national interests generally have prevailed against cooperative efforts (see
Lauber in this volume).
     Individual countries have to be examined to see how
these policies have differed. France has pursued largely interventionist policies, while Great Britain has
pursued protectionist policies. In contrast, West Germany has relied more on the free market and was one of
the early supporters of a general (or European) industrial policy. The smaller nations of Europe also have
pursued differing industrial policies. Several of the

Scandinavian countries, particularly Sweden, have developed some of the most comprehensive policies. Austria, too, has developed a more comprehensive industrial policy than have most other European nations. Thus, industrial policies vary greatly among European nations.

What accounts for these wide differences in industrial policy among the nations of Europe and between them and the United States? The contributors to this volume posit a variety of reasons: the political culture and ideology of nations, the roles of interest groups and political parties, the political structure of the governments themselves, and the nature of particular policies or sectors of a nation's domestic and international economy. All of these have important influence on what types of policies will result.

Beginning with ideology, it is clear from public opinion data and the contributors to this volume that there is greater consensus for government intervention in what are supposedly "strictly economic" issues in some countries (e.g., Japan) than others (e.g., the United States). Largely because of the wide differences within the varied European nations, there has been little consensus as to whether there should be a comprehensive industrial policy for the European Community (EC).

A nation's ideology is closely related to the role of nongovernmental institutions. American society, of course, is often considered among the world's most pluralistic and heterogeneous; thus, little consensus should be expected over major government intervention (see Lawrence in this volume). Not surprisingly, in the less pluralized nations such as Japan, Sweden, and Austria, consensually-based policies have appeared more frequently. Large-scale nonincremental changes, which are usual in the imposition of industrial policies, are therefore much less likely in the United States (see Peters in this volume).

The widely differeing roles of interest groups and political parties illustrate the significance of a nation's ideology. Unionization is a more dominant influence in governmental decision making in Europe than in the United States, where other interest groups compete with labor. The greater number of decision points, i.e., decentralization, of the decision-making process in the United States allows many different groups considerable access. Pelinka shows the diversity of unionization within Europe, where labor is more centralized and integrated into the political system in Sweden than in Great Britain and France. He suggests that fragmentation in Great Britain has limited the impact of labor and is a possible reason why that country is not doing as well economically as Sweden.

The cohesiveness of political parties is also an important condition in whether nations will develop comprehensive public policies. Not only are political parties more cohesive in Europe than in the United States but the competing European parties offer the public a wider variety of policy options.

However, despite the frequent charge that American parties offer the public only trivially different policy options, the following case study illustrates that differences have occurred over industrial policy in recent years. The two major U.S. parties have adopted opposing stances which reflect their differing constituencies and perhaps even "ideologies." Republicans traditionally favor free trade but also recognize that the trade issue is not so simple. Economist Herbert Stein (1983) observes, "every American president denies that he is protectionist, but presidents differ in the degree to which they are prepared to make exceptions" (p. 3). The Reagan administration's fiscal and monetary policies did not create a favorable climate for U.S. exports (Rohatyn, 1984). High interest rates and an overvalued dollar made U.S. goods expensive abroad and foreign goods relatively cheap at home. The result in the early 1980s was a sharp decline in U.S. exports and growing trade deficits. The Reagan administration was prepared to tolerate the strong dollar and declining exports to achieve other economic goals. For instance, they responded to calls for protection for autos, motorcycles, and steel, but have resisted demands for protection in other areas. Phillips (1984) believes that it may "take a proven foe of government activism Reagan to bring about real collaboration between government and business" (p. 23).

The Democratic party, in search of alternatives to the Republicans' supply-side approach, has been receptive to proposals for a new industrial policy. Robert Reich's books were required reading for the Democratic contenders in 1984. Discussions of industrial policy figured in preparation of the 1984 Democratic platform but received little attention in the subsequent campaign, largely because major divisions developed among the Democrats themselves (National Journal, September 29, 1984, p. 1829).

However, dissents from both right and left have appeared. Former Council of Economic Advisors Chairman, Charles L. Schultze (1983), challenges the potential of an industrial policy. He argues that the U.S. industrial base has not decliend but, in fact, has been significantly diversified in the past decade. Further, Schultze challenges the real impact of the Ministry of International Trade and Industry (MITI) in Japan. He claims that not only is it impossible for the government to pick the proper "mix" of industries for a country, but to try to do so would be disastrous.

Some conservatives also reject calls for an industrial policy. Arthur Denzau (1983) echoes Schultze's
doubt about the success of MITI and the Japanese industrial program. He suggests that an industrial policy
in the United States would be dominated by those firms
with existing power in the political system--automobile
and steel manufacturers--with backing from big unions as
well as big business. Denzau concludes that industrial
policy would lead to "the institutionalization of piecemeal protectionism of the sort we now have"(1983, p.13).

American society is highly decentralized--not only
with separation of powers among the governing branches
but among levels of government as well (i.e., national,
state, local). The many actors and decision points in
American politics contribute to the lack of consensus
discussed above. A corporatist political structure,
like Austria's, makes comprehensive, consensual industrial policy decisions easier (see Pelinka in this
volume). These different structural conditions facilitate very different kinds of policies.

POLICY CONTENT

Scholars debate whether industrial policy is primarily
foreign or domestic, economic or political. It is
argued here that industrial policy is more a political
than an economic decision. It is a conscious governmental action or intervention taken upon the inability of
economic (market) forces to bring about desired public
policy outcomes. Because industrial policy contains
elements of all of the above types, it has been difficult to classify, categorize, or even define. Upon first
examination, industrial policy seems to be primarily an
economic issue dealing with international trade. Obviously, it has foreign policy implications affecting relationships among nations and challenges to dominant
ideologies. But whether or not to have an industrial
policy and the shape it may take also would have domestic implications: the degree the nation subsidizes declining interests, accedes to union demands, retrains
workers, and becomes involved in a host of other social
and political issues. Industrial policy is just one of
many issue areas that shows the interrelationship of
foreign and domestic policy and how economics has
blurred its traditional distinctions (Blumenthal, 1978,
p. 738; Hoffman, 1977, p. 48; LeLoup and Shull, 1979).
The need for industrial policies is one example of growing global economic and political interdependencies.

Industrial policy is tied to foreign trade (e.g.,
how much protectionism and tariffs one can impose) and
also to the problem of economic disruptions (e.g., how
and whether to protect declining regions/industries or
to spur new ones). The latter questions raise serious

social and political as well as economic concerns (Dolbeare, 1984). Inevitably, a nation's ideology and politics influence its relations with other nations; and industrial policies illustrate this important nexus between
economics and politics. At the same time, different sub-
issues within industrial policy are differentially affected by government intervention (e.g., steel vs. autos).
Therefore, some say that it makes more sense to discuss
such components or sectors of industrial policy.

Despite the ambiguities of determining just what industrial policy means, all nations have industrial policies if only at the sector level. Even the United States
has industrial policies; not a comprehensive one, but
policies for particular industries (e.g., subsidizing
transportation, regulating communication). Peters is of
the opinion that the United States has too many divergent
specific policies and that we have not yet decided the
extent we wish to target policies or what goals we seek
to accomplish.

If government responses in the United States have
been largely sector oriented, so have those of European
governments. Nation-specific protectionism has been particularly strong with regard to automobiles and agriculture while greater cooperation among European nations
has occurred in other areas, mainly steel production in
recent years. During the 1980s, there began to be numerous cooperative ventures across European borders. The
United States is also increasing its cooperative ventures
in space exploration. Such policies are increasing despite scholars' inabilities in demarcating substantive
typologies.

One may also categorize policy according to functional areas. The most famous categorization scheme, offered
by Lowi (1964), is that of distributive, regulatory, and
redistributive policy. Distributive policies primarily
affect specific, homogeneous groups, arise from relatively narrow issues, and provide mostly individualized,
short-run benefits. Distributive policies are not very
visible, which results in little conflict in the policy
process. Regulatory policies involve the application of
general rules to specific decisions. Sanctions, restrictions, and coercion characterize regulatory policies although benefits may also be conferred. Regulations tend
to involve broad extensions of governmental control that
affect large elements of society. Redistributive policies
allocate benefits and impose costs by taking assets from
one group and giving them to another. These policies
generally have the broadest impact on society. Redistributive policies often alienate powerful interests, are
highly visible and conflictual, and one finds high levels
of presidential participation. The president is less
involved in the other functional areas where Congress
dominates.

These definitional characteristics seem to place
industrial policy squarely within the redistributive
classification. Peters thinks it is inherently so, yet
he writes of the general preference for distributive
policies in the United States. We know that Congress is
almost invariably so inclined, and the fragmented nature
of policymaking in America makes the distributive type
of policy most common. On the other hand, redistributive policies are much more common in Europe, where
there is a more corporatist mentality and greater willingness for government intervention to aid the "general
welfare."

An irony in this situation is that most sectoral
policies in the United States are redistributive, perhaps more so than a general industrial policy might be.
A comprehensive policy for the United States would inevitably be more distributive and incremental, while
helping a depressed industry would have an immediate impact on specific sectors. Accordingly, industrial policy cuts across conventional policy types, whether substantive or functional. Peters, Cohen and Brunk, Pelinka, and others discuss this redistributive aspect of
industrial policymaking.

We have discussed the blurring of economic concerns
into industrial policy. We see this blurring when attempting to apply the functional typology to industrial
policy. In the United States, we find forces trying to
transform redistributive elements of industrial policy
into a more distributive policy. The geographic alloca-
tion of benefits, which is a policy option that Congress
usually prefers, is one indication of these forces at
work (see Peters in this volume). The piecemeal approach
to industrial sectors also illustrates the impact of
distributive forces in the United States. Yet, while
Europe's response may be more comprehensive and redistributive within nations, the inability to foster strong
EC cooperation in all but a few industries reveals some
distributive forces at work in Europe as well (see
Pelinka in this volume). However, the standard functional typology seems less useful in explaining industrial policy than it has been in explaining older policies. This may derive from the transformation of various discrete economic problems into what we now call
industrial policy, with its linkages between economic
sectors and the macroeconomy, and between domestic,
foreign, and trade policy.

THE CONTRIBUTIONS TO THIS VOLUME

All the essays in this volume recognize the importance
of relationships among policy actors (both governmental
and nongovernmental) as well as among policy areas in
the determination of whether industrial policies will

be formulated and implemented. Despite the widely differing roles of actors and implementation of industrial
policy in Europe and the United States, these roles are
extremely important as Olson (1985) dramatically reveals.

The keynote presentation by Robert Lawrence points
out that all nations have a "type of industrial policy"
designed to allocate production and labor and encourage
research and development. Lawrence focuses on four
propositions others have raised about whether the United
States needs an industrial policy. The first refers to
perceived flaws in U.S. manufacturing: a concern for
short-term profits rather than long-term planning.
Lawrence disputes this contention by arguing that "poor
manufacturing performance cannot be explained in terms
of failure to invest." The second charge, primarily by
Reich (1983), is that foreigners have more farsighted
managers. Lawrence counters this by observing that the
United States shows greater increases in the proportion
of employment in high tech industries than either West
Germany or Japan. Besides, spending in the United
States for research and development--even outside the
defense areas--recently has been increasing faster than
inflation. The third proposition is that the interna-
tionalization of the U.S. economy highlights our economic difficulties. Lawrence believes that the strongest explanation for U.S. economic problems involve domestic taxing and spending policies. Finally, he addresses the question of whether structural deficiencies
account for the erosion of the U.S. manufacturing base.
He sees some structural problems but, again, believes
that many of our problems are macroeconomic in nature
and, thus, require macroeconomic solutions.

While Lawrence's essay primarily discusses whether
there should be an industrial policy in the United
States, it has important implications for Europe as
well. He argues that European countries have the advantage of looking at the example of more technologically developed countries, like Japan and the United States
and learning from their mistakes. Despite having much
more central planning, European nations are still playing catch-up, at least on the frontier of new high technology industrialization (see also Lawrence, 1984).

Both of our essays on Europe show that, to the extent industrial policies exist, they are country specific: there is no "European" industrial policy but,
rather, enormous diversity exists. Volkmar Lauber
points to the major differences among the European nations. Both general responses and economic sector responses vary. Lauber reveals how individualistic national policies have totally undermined solidarity in
the European Community. He notes that there is no EC
policy, not even in old industries (except perhaps in
steel) let alone in the emerging growth industries.

Lauber concludes that the "goal of unification remains
as remote today as it was two decades ago." He sees
several reasons why there is no common industrial policy in Europe: differing national interests, conflicting ideologies, fear of supranationality, insufficient
resources, and constitutional restrictions. Despite
such difficulties, Lauber sees increased transnational
cooperation in the 1980s.

Anton Pelinka also sees great contrasts across
European industrial policies. He recognizes that industrial policy is a mixture of political and economic
systems.* He suggests that "industrial democracy" fits
between the extremes of a structured market economy and
a centrally planned economy. Pelinka develops and
tests two hypotheses about a broader concept he calls
"neocorporatism"--industrial democracy above the corporate level. The organization of unions is an important variable in both propositions. Pelinka finds that
the "entry of unions into the...power center...is an
unconditional necessity for the development of neocorporatism as industrial democracy." Although he thinks
there should be a European standard, Pelinka recognizes
that European diversity makes it unlikely in the near
future.

The Cohen and Brunk and the Peters essays stress
the importance of ideology, interest groups, and political parties as influencing the economy where all experts recognize that relative economic decline has occurred in America.

Jeffrey Cohen and Gregory Brunk test elements of
Mancur Olson's (1982) theory that interest groups hamper economic growth by looking not at the nation as a
whole but at the individual states. They consider several variables that may influence economic growth: the
extent of urbanization, unionization (Pelinka's main
variable), and the age and location of a state. While
none of the empirical tests of Olson's theory to date
have been definitive, Cohen and Brunk find some support
for Olson's assertion that stronger interest groups are
related to economic decline. They also posit political
party strength as an alternative explanation but found
that where parties were a major factor on economic policy in Europe (Lauber, Pelinka), parties in the American
states had no effect on economic growth after accounting
for the effects of interest groups. Their essay provides a useful extension of Olson's important theory and
also relates to diffusion within the United States, a
topic of concern to Peters.

Guy Peters thinks regional diversity is part of the
reason why the United States has not adopted a comprehensive industrial policy. Other related reasons include

_____

*Recall that politics and economics are more close-
ly intertwined in Europe than in the United States.

ideology, parochial imperatives, institutions, incrementalism, and economic structure. Congress as well as
state and local governments leans toward distributive
policies (Lowi, 1972; Shull, 1983) whereas an integrated industrial policy for America would clearly be redistributive (support particular industries/regions at
the expense of others). Because Americans are concerned
greatly about equity among all producers and regions,
Peters thinks a comprehensive industrial policy is unlikely and probably also undesirable. Like Cohen and
Brunk, Peters discusses the fragmented but important
role of interest groups in American policymaking. He
believes that interest groups could be incorporated
more formally into decision making to help coordinate
economic policy.

The conclusion to this volume draws implications
from the papers and panel discussions presented at the
seventh biannual symposium. It summarizes views about
whether industrial policy is successful in Europe and
feasible in the United States. The focus is largely on
the American scene, however, where numerous reform prospects are considered. Most of our authors would like
to see market forces prevail almost exclusively. Still,
while recognizing the inherent difficulties they believe limited changes or reforms may halt America's
economic decline if not develop a comprehensive industrial policy. While interventionist policies that are
heavily protectionist are not favored, worker retraining is considered a legitimate government enterprise.
Thus, it is believed that, even in the United States,
government may need to take a greater leadership role
than it has heretofore--that is, to use politics to
counter economic and social disruption.

If there is an overarching theme to this volume,
it is that politics pervades industrial policymaking
not only in the United States but elsewhere. The essays reveal the interrelationship among actors and policies. Beginning first with actors, they contrast the
relative role of governmental and nongovernmental participants in policymaking. Interest groups seemingly
are a more powerful influence on industrial policy decisions in the United States, while parties dominate in
Europe. Yet labor, the major European interest group,
is becoming weaker in the United States while single-
issue interest groups are growing in influence.

Researchers are faced with intractable measurement
problems. Cohen and Brunk reveal the difficulties of
specifying indicators and the need for dynamic rather
than static research designs. They admit that unionization, for example, may not be as good an indicator of
interest group strength in the United States as it is
in Europe. National goals are also hard to determine
as are the motives for such policies as "picking winners."

Scholars must be sensitive to the levels of analysis problems because the extent of industrial policies varies enormously depending upon whether one is discussing supranational or subnational public policies. Finally, it is not always clear what researchers mean by industrial policies; but it is argued here that it may help if they are placed within the broader context and content of public policy.

2
Myths and Realities on America's Need for an Industrial Policy

Robert Z. Lawrence

During 1982, as the United States' economy moved into
its deepest postwar recession, there arose some notions
that the economy's problems extended far deeper than
those that could be attributed simply to an economic recession. From 1979 to 1982, employment in the American
manufacturing sector had plummeted by about 10.5 percent. In addition, partly as a result of the strong
dollar, the international trade balance of manufactured
products in the economy had eroded significantly.

These developments produced a heightened concern
and a re-examination of what caused the poor performance
of the American manufacturing sector. Some suggested
that the United States required a new industrial policy.
In my view, the phrase industrial policy is extremely
broad and almost meaningless as it stands. It must be
given some content before one can have a reasonable discussion. Industrial policy refers to policies which
the government undertakes in order to influence the al-
location of resources in the economy.

I would first like to classify the notion of industrial policy in several ways. Industrial policy
should be distinguished from macroeconomic policies,
which are policies that influence the supply of money
in the economy, the overall levels of taxation and government spending, and they significantly affect the al-
location of resources.

In termsof the more precise microeconomic policies,
all of which can be classified as industrial policies,
it makes sense to note some distinctions. First, there
are policies which are designed for a specific factor of
production. Policies affecting labor, for example, include unemployment insurance and training and relocation
programs. These general policies are applied to all
workers and can be thought of as horizontal industrial
policies. We also have a second set of policies designed
to encourage research and development throughout the entire economy. For example, the investment tax credit
available to all corporations in this country creates

15

incentives for investment in research and development. Again, these are horizontal policies applied to all industries. A third group of policies focuses on capital formation. Accelerated depreciation allowances, for example, are used to promote investment.

In addition to macro- and micropolicies, there exist general policies that establish rules. In the domestic arena we have antitrust regulations, while in the international arena we have the GATT rules to regulate the global trading system. Aside from these general policies, there are industry specific policies. The most noteworthy of such policies in the United States occur in agriculture, an industry with its own specific set of policies. Nuclear energy is another example.

The United States has a vast array of industrial policies, but to ask whether it needs an overall industrial policy is to ask the wrong question; every economy has these groups of policies. I think, however, advocates of a new industrial policy for the United States are suggesting something quite different. Their suggestions contain elements of general or horizontal policies as well as the idea that the United States should make policy on an industry-by-industry basis. In so doing, the United States could more effectively coordinate its economic policies and improve its industrial performance.

What distinguishes the new suggestions, though, is an idea which I would like to divide into two components: (1) the government should design an ideal industrial structure, and (2) the government should use the array of instruments at its disposal, such as trade policy, regulatory policy, and government procurement to bring about that structure. Some people say that the government should not design such a plan and, therefore, industrial policy is not synonomous with economic planning. However, they suggest that a tripartite board composed of representatives of government, labor, and academia should be assigned the task of determining an ideal structure. Others are reluctant to get involved in great detail in planning a structure, and suggest that the government select and support certain kinds of activities, such as high technology or industries with high value added. Nonetheless, new notions of American industry's behavior and new policies toward U.S. industrial performance have been advanced.

Three questions that relate to these proposals must be addressed before attempting to determine the type of industrial policy the United States ought to have:

1. What are the major sources of the economic difficulty that the U.S. manufacturing sector has experienced over the past few years? Are they fundamentally structural problems which ought to be dealt with by a

new set of industrial policies, or do they perhaps reflect other problems which may be more appropriately
dealt with using, for example, macroeconomic policies?

2. Assuming that some of the problems in this economy and in manufacturing performance require new policies, what kinds of policies in principle should be considered.

3. What kind of policies will work best in our economy in practice, given our political and social institutions? What may work in Austria, Japan, or in other economies may not be appropriate for the United States.

In response to the first question, an array of fundamental problems have been conceived. The literature
contains four types of propositions put forth by proponents of a U.S. industrial policy.

1. The first idea is that there was something fundamentally wrong with the way American manufacturing was
performing, although there was no consensus on an explanation for this. Some blamed management for not being willing to plow back profits into long-term projects. Other
observers designated the government as the major source
of the problem, although here they propounded that U.S.
problems stemmed from too much government. Through ex-
cessive regulation and trade protection, the government
had inhibited the market forces, thereby reducing capital formation, savings, and productivity. The appropriate policy, therefore, was simply for the government to
get out of the way. On the other hand, another group believed that government intervention had been of the wrong
kind. The U.S. economy needed a new strategy. Industries
with growth potential should be promoted and industries
going into decline should be assisted, the individuals
dislocated from such industries should be helped to find
other employment opportunities.

2. A second notion the industrial policy proponents
emphasized was that foreigners did not suffer to the same
degree from these problems. Indeed, foreign management
tended to be more farsighted and willing to reinvest.
Labor and management apparently had less of an adversari-
al relationship. Foreign governments appeared to have
strategies designed to promote industries of the future
and to assist declining industries. This comparison contrasted the inherent difficulties in the U.S. mechanism
and method of manufacturing performance with superior
foreign methods.

3. The third notion was that, through increased
trade over the 1970s, the inherent U.S. difficulties
were exposed. During the 1970s, a rapid international-
ization of the U.S. economy highlighted these difficulties which had not been as obvious in prior years.

4. Primarily as a result of international trade,
structural change in the U.S. economy had become increasingly difficult to accomplish. Indeed, many believed

that as a result of trade (which reflected the inherent difficulties), America as a whole was deindustrializing. In other words, the manufacturing base of the country was eroding.

These four major propositions were contained in a number of critiques, and were the motivating factors which promoted the arguments that we ought to have a new industrial policy.

In the course of my study, I examined the evidence concerning these propositions (Lawrence, 1984). Was there compelling evidence of a deep flaw in the U.S. manufacturing process? Was there compelling evidence that trade was a major factor in structural change in the U.S. economy? Was the structural dislocation in the economy immensely greater than what had occurred in previous periods? To answer these questions, one must account for the effect of the general macroeconomic developments in the economy. After all, in 1982 the U.S. economy was experiencing a deep recession. Was the unemployment experienced in the U.S. manufacturing sector, over the period 1979 to 1982, more than one would have expected given the overall state of the economy? In my analysis I discovered that the amount of unemployment in our manufacturing sector was almost exactly what one would expect. By relating employment performance in the American manufacturing sector to what had happened in the overall U.S. economy between 1973 and 1980, again there was no mystery. Employment performed exactly as one would have expected. This fact is also true of the economic recovery since 1982. Indeed, employment in the manufacturing sector of the United States has not reached its 1979 peak, but is well on its way and more than two-thirds has been regained.

The U.S. economy continues to behave very much in accordance with historical experience. I find this surprising because over the same period between 1982 and 1984, we have experienced a tremendous erosion in the international trade performance of the United States. In my view, this performance is fundamentally related to the strength of our currency. Indeed, numerous statistical tests that we have done suggest that there is no surprise in explaining why U.S. imports have increased by 60 percent and exports have decreased by 20 percent since 1980 (Lawrence, 1984, pp. 45-50). These movements have resulted primarily from what has happened to the price of our goods as compared to those of our competitors; but they are not primarily related to the differences in our industrial policies.

Despite the massive erosion in our international trade performance, the overall behavior of the U.S. manufacturing sector is normal for an economic recovery. One would not expect a sector negatively affected by the strong dollar to experience normal recovery. So how

has this normal recovery been possible? Two offsetting
sources of strength exist in the U.S. economy which
have compensated the manufacturing sector. A minor
factor is the increase in defense procurement of equipment goods which stimulate manufacturing production.
But, more important, an abnormally large amount of
equipment spending has occurred. This spending includes
purchases of automobiles and trucks, office equipment,
and machinery. In the U.S. postwar recovery periods,
the amount of equipment spending in the first two years
grew at the rate of 18 or 19 percent. In this recovery,
however, equipment spending grew by 40 percent. Employment in the U.S. automobile industry today stands at
920,000. At its peak in 1979 it reached 1 million, so
our auto employment has dropped by 8 percent (Lawrence,
1984, pp. 45-50). In the trough of the recession, employment was at 700,000 which represented a 30 percent
decline from the 1979 peak; however, 22 percent of that
decline has already been recovered (Lawrence, 1984, p.
34).

In my judgment, if the economy can sustain its economic growth, the overall manufacturing sector will continue to perform as it has in the past and normal recovery will proceed. That is not to imply that nothing
is wrong with the behavior of our manufacturing sector;
but, nonetheless, no significant evidence confirms that
the United States has in this sense been deindustrializing or that our manufacturing base has been eroded in
the aggregate. Although some industries are in trouble,
it is not evident that, on the whole, our economy has
experienced deindustrialization.

The second issue involves the idea that foreigners
have conscious policies which allocate resources into
the industries of the future and withdraw them from the
industries of the past, whereas the United States has no
such policies. This idea is the central argument of
Robert Reich's book, The Next American Frontier (1983).
Reich argues that the fundamental problem with the U.S.
manufacturing sector is performance; we are not creating
enough jobs for the future.

The United States has not had a conscious policy of
cultivating particular kinds of industries. Rather than
listening to policymakers' claims of what they are doing,
we should consider the actual structural change occurring
in the U.S. economy. If we compare the structural change
in the United States with that of West Germany and Japan,
we find that since 1973 there has been a greater increase
in the share of employment in the United States in high
technology industries. The proportion of our manufacturing sector shifting into the high technology group is
far greater than that in Japan and West Germany (Lawrence,
1984, p. 34). Looking at the labor-intensive industries
of the past, such as apparel, textiles, and furniture,
we find that these industries had the greatest decline

in West Germany which has withdrawn from the industries
of the past more rapidly than the United States or
Japan. The ability of the U.S. economy to move to the
high technology industries--the industries of the fu-
ture--reveals the extent of flexibility in our industrial sector.

A third proposition was the notion that the United
States has failed to invest sufficiently in research
and development or capital formation. This failure to
invest, they claim, has produced competitive problems
in the manufacturing sector. Much of the data used to
support this argument, however, relates to the U.S.
economy as a whole. Since 1973, the capital:labor ratio
has not grown as rapidly in the United States as in
other countries. Indeed, this was a major motivation
behind the design of the Reagan economic package to encourage investment. In the manufacturing sector of the
U.S. economy, however, since 1973 investment increased
at a much more rapid rate than it had in earlier periods.
In addition, between 1975 and 1980, the U.S. manufacturing sector increased as rapidly as capital accumulation.
Employment increased in the services sector while capital went into the manufacturing sector. A close examination of the data reveals that we cannot explain poor
manufacturing performance in terms of a failure to invest. To a certain extent, our poor overall economic
performance may have been attributable to our investing
behavior, but that was not true in the manufacturing
sector.

Another alleged difficulty related to capital is
American business myopia. Although it is very difficult
to quantify the effects of this myopia, one indicator
would be research and development spending. If business
were not interested in the future, the marked accelera-
tion in research and development spending in this country since 1978 would not have occurred. Comparing the
expenditures financed by private U.S. corporations
since 1978 with expenditures financed by the Pentagon
illustrates how rapid the rise was. The Europeans tend
to make much of the role of defense in our research and
development in explaining U.S. industrial performance.
It is important to realize that since 1978, however,
private spending on research and development has increased at the same rate as research and development
financed by the government for defense purposes--about
6.5 percent a year. We are experiencing a rapid reju-
venation in expenditures on research and development
financed primarily by U.S. business. I believe that defense has been a major component in U.S. industrial policies, but during the 1970s in particular there was a
tremendous cutback in R&D going on in the defense sector.
So, to explain American performance in the 1980s, we can
not consider defense. Primarily what we are seeing today
in the U.S. economy is not related to defense spending.

In order to determine the effect trade has had on the American manufacturing sector, we have to consider trade before and after 1980 to reflect the differences in the behavior of the U.S. dollar (Lawrence, 1984, pp. 38-50). For the period before 1980, I asked the question: How many jobs can the U.S. manufacturing sector create as a result of export growth? And, then, how many jobs are lost as a result of increased imports of manufactured products? By totaling the results, one can estimate the effect trade has had on the size of employment in the American manufacturing sector. (Recall that a major thesis of those who suggest that we need an industrial policy is that trade is deindustrializing the U.S. economy.) I found that over the course of the 1970s, as many jobs were created in American manufacturing as a result of the growth of exports as were lost as a result of the rise in imports. This came as a great surprise to me because I anticipated a different conclusion. I tried to ask myself why there was the impression throughout the U.S. economy, even in 1980, that trade was having such a negative effect. To answer this question, I compared the employment changes in the U.S. economy that were due to other factors, and I broke these down by industry. I found that the industries which tended to do relatively well in international trade were the same ones that experienced greater growth as a result of what was happening in the domestic economy. These were the high technology industries. High technology industries experienced strong growth because of domestic factors and international trade. On the other hand, the industries with slow domestic growth, i.e., the basic industries, experienced lower gains and, in some cases, losses resulting from international trade. Because Americans saw certain industries in difficulty and those same industries also had problems in their international trade, they assumed causation between these two phenomenon.

The overwhelming reasons for structural change in the U.S. economy remain domestic in origin. The automobile industry provides an appropriate illustration. Most Americans believe that the reason the United States has unemployment in its auto industry is the increase in the purchases of Japanese automobiles. In fact, two reasons exist for this problem: (1) Americans were buying fewer cars; (2) of the cars they were buying, more of them were of Japanese manufacture. Therefore, Japanese purchases assumed a greater share of the market. However, had Americans bought the same number of cars but bought only American cars, about 80 percent of the workers would still have lost their jobs. Only 20 percent of the unemployment can be attributed to the fact that Americans bought more Japanese cars (Lawrence, 1984, pp. 55-61). This fact points to the crucial idea that the overwhelming source of the structural change of the

general unemployment of the U.S. economy was related to
the domestic economy. I think that the recovery illustrates a similar phenomenon.

International trade is important and growing in importance, but a fundamental difference between the U.S.
and the Austrian economies is the degree to which the
United States remains relatively self-contained. Over-
whelmingly, the forces at work stem from our domestic
economy. Sometimes changes brought about by international trade reinforce the changes occurring in the domestic economy. We are increasingly becoming a high
technology-based economy. At the same time, U.S. ex-
porters of high technology goods do relatively better
than those of basic manufactured goods. So trade is a
reinforcing factor, but the overwhelming source of the
structural change remains domestic in origin.

Prior to 1980, the employment effects of trade
were equal. The manufacturing sector was not being de-
industrialized, it was experiencing slow growth primarily because of what happened in the overall economy.
This finding indicated the crucial need for macroeconomic policies designed to stimulate growth. Since 1980,
I believe that the overwhelming reason for our poor
trade performance relates to strength in the dollar.
There is a direct link between the strong dollar and
U.S. macroeconomic policy, especially budgetary policy.
More specifically, a direct link exists between our fiscal deficit and our trade deficit. If an economy
reaches full employment, what happens if the government
increases its spending relative to its income? One of
two outcomes will result: either the private citizens
must change their spending habits to lend the money to
the government, or the money has to be obtained from
abroad. The U.S. economy has a large structural deficit
that will persist, even at full employment. Private
citizens have not changed their spending patterns and,
therefore, a large portion of the deficit is met by bor-
rowing from abroad. The trade deficit implies that the
country spends more than it earns. A trade deficit is
fundamentally a macroeconomic problem and must be dealt
with by changing fiscal policies through both tax and
expenditure policies. Trade policies cannot change the
overall trade deficit.

What kind of principles should the United States
follow if policymakers choose to implement an industrial
policy? Proponents of U.S. industrial policies frequently deny that they seek to pick winners and losers.
And yet, they suggest that the United States ought to
have as one instrument of policy a national bank to provide loans to industries. This policy would shift the
responsibility of choosing winners or losers from planners to bankers. What criteria would the bankers use?
This is an extremely difficult question to answer because

the real issue is not whether the United States needs a
steel industry, that is an easy question to answer, we
do need some kind of a steel industry. The question is
how large should the U.S. steel industry be? Should the
next dollar that we spend go into steel, or into some
other industry? How can we efficiently allocate our resources? The crucial point is that efficiency involves
decisions at the margin. Although many engineers enter
high technology industry, we may be better off encourag-
ing engineers to go into a basic industry to help re-
store its competitiveness. What makes achieving efficiency so difficult is that we are at the technological
frontier. We do not have a clear notion of where growth
is going to come.

   This is a crucial difference between our economy
and European economies up until recently and, indeed,
the developing economies. The European and developing
economies have the advantage of observing more developed
countries to see the pattern along which these economies
evolved. For example, if a country is going to indus-
trialize successfully, it will improve its agricultural
system, improve its textile industry, and then develop
basic steel, then automobiles, and then technology. When
an economy such as the United States is on the technological frontier, it is far more difficult to know where
the breakthroughs are going to come. A country may be
able to centralize, to plan, and to facilitate and ac-
celerate change when its economy is catching up, but
when its economy is on the frontier, different kinds of
policies are appropriate. For the United States, we do
not know at the margin where the next dollars ought to
be spent. I am fundamentally skeptical of a frontier
economy's ability to allocate resources in a centralized
fashion. I believe that, to some degree, the fundamental European tendency to overgeneralize stems from the
fact that they have a catch-up economy, while Americans
are dealing with a frontier economy. In a catch-up
economy, one can be certain of its rate of productivity
growth and predetermine the kinds of industries that
will continue to grow. The government finds it easy to
make guarantees and to proclaim that it will preserve
certain kinds of jobs. Businessmen find it easy to know
where the future will lie. It is, therefore, possible
to be more farsighted in investment decisions. But in
a frontier economy, the risk is far greater. In my
view, the reason that the U.S. economy has performed better in the era of slow global growth and of post oil
shock disturbances since 1973 has been precisely because
it has always been a frontier economy and, therefore, it
has always had to be more flexible. U.S. businessmen
had to learn how to guard themselves against numerous
recessions, and this is why U.S. equity markets developed.
The American public has learned to bear greater risks.

The kind of social guarantees provided in the U.S. economy were much lower than those provided in the European context. Again, this results from the fact that in an economy which has great uncertainty it is much more difficult to make such guarantees. As the world economy has become more uncertain, the European institutions have had greater difficulty in adjusting. They lack flexibility in their economies, their equity markets are underdeveloped, and innovation is difficult. Their overall social structures have been appropriate for catch-up economies. The United States has not performed exceptionally well over the last decade compared to its historical record, but it has been less affected by the uncertainties in the world economy because it has a more flexible economy.

Let me say further that I am quite skeptical of other arguments that explain why we ought to have industrial policies. One is that we need certain industries for national defense purposes. Another is that we are losing certain kinds of middle income job opportunities in our economy. Industrial policies--policies dealing with individual industries--are extremely inefficient ways of achieving such objectives as enhancing the national defense or changing the distribution of income. Economic policies should be targeted precisely. I believe that certain kinds of activities are necessary for national defense. The way to preserve those is to give a certain amount of money to the defense planners, and require them to buy the best defense available. If the United States needs a certain industrial capacity or, indeed, if it needs certain research and development capabilities, the defense budget should be used to pay for these. We should not use trade policy indirectly to preserve some industry for national defense purposes. This is bound to be an inefficient policy. Chrysler Corporation has a tank division which may be essential for national defense. If so, the tank division should be subsidized instead of maintaining the entire auto industry or firm in the name of national defense. Policies must be targeted precisely.

Another example of how imprecision has affected the U.S. economy involves poor farmers. If we are worried about poor farmers, we should give them money; that is the most precise method of implementing a policy. Instead, the United States has a policy for the whole agricultural sector. This is a tremendously inefficient policy. The richer the farmer, the more the output and, thus, the greater amount of money he receives. Instead of directly targeting the program to deal with the problem, we have indirectly tried to solve it by involving an entire industry.

Another example concerns income distribution in our economy. If we believe that the middle class has been eroded, the appropriate policy approach is to redistribute

income using the tax system. If we are worried about
poverty, we should directly target poverty. If we are
worried about certain regions, we should directly target
those regions. We should not be moving through the in-
termediate vehicle of dealing with industries in order
to achieve these objectives. Recall yet another example
of U.S. policy failure because the policy dealt with industries, even though the concern was for regions. In
the 1960s, we worried about the New England region and
the state of its textile industry. We protected the entire textile industry to mitigate the difficulties occurring in New England. The intent of the program was
to save jobs. The textile industry migrated from New
England to the south and, in the 1970s, that new textile
industry in the south needed protection. Workers were
the motivation behind our policies, but they were not
precisely targeted. We simply protected an entire industry.

Appropriate industrial policies for the United
States are horizontal policies rather than those that
deal with industries. We ought to have a policy encour-
aging research and development, but this policy should
be broadly available throughout our economy. I think
that we can improve our approaches to labor market adjustment. We should assist dislocated workers rather
than trying to prevent dislocation by dealing with
these problems on an industry-by-industry basis.

In the U.S. context, before moving into more interventionist policies, we also have to examine our political system. We looked into the countries where industrial policies have worked and those where they have been
unsuccessful. In the countries where they have not
worked, the crucial difference remains the amount of
consensus that surrounds the particular policies. Industrial policies are long-term policies. If we were,
for instance, to open an investment bank in this country, it would take five years to establish it and to allocate the money, and fifteen years before we would
know if it were succeeding or not. That kind of policy
could take place only where a broad national consensus
existed. In countries like France or Japan there is a
strong consensus about what must be done and a strong
acceptance of detailed industrial policies. In Great
Britain, there has been no such strong consensus, resulting in alternating policies and great uncertainty.

In America today, little consensus exists behind
detailed interventionist policies. Even if such policies were to be implemented, I think that businesses
would suspect that within four or five years the policies would be changed. The United States must improve
its structural policies in areas where there is a broad
consensus. In general, these are areas in which most
recognize that private markets fail. Only in such areas
should we have detailed policies. For example, we have

strong reasons to believe that in some areas private
markets cannot be as effective as the government, i.e.,
the inventor does not get all the benefits of his invention; the benefits to society are much greater.
Therefore, we should promote research and development
to compensate for this market failure. Another example
is training and education. I cannot go to a bank and
get a loan sufficient to finance my education at Harvard
University, even though everyone knows that Harvard is
a great investment. Because the market fails to provide such loans, the government serves a purpose in
this area. The problem is that the poor student has
no collateral to provide for the loan. The government
can collect the loan more easily than can the bank.

Let me close by saying that I believe that much of
the difficulty experienced in the U.S. economy can be
attributed to macroeconomic sources and requires a macroeconomic solution. Nonetheless, there remains scope
for improving our structural programs, and I think
there is a consensus in this country to improve these
programs on a broader basis. Many fewer people favor
and a weaker argument exists for using industry-specific
policies.

3
The Political Economy of Industrial Policy in Western Europe

*Volkmar Lauber**

The European Community formulates its industrial policy at different levels.[1] Most of it originates with the national governments of the member countries, but in some cases regional or local authorities are the prime policymakers. There have been several attempts to establish policies for the Community as a whole although success has been limited. There is a strong contrast between the practice of selective intervention within the member states and a rather liberal reliance on the market at the level of the Community, at least in the area of industrial as opposed to agricultural policy. This essay compares industrial policy in Europe on the Community and the national levels.

INDUSTRIAL POLICY ON THE COMMUNITY LEVEL

Industrial policy has been the subject of much debate at the Community level, but of little practice; only isolated elements of it exist. This situation is parallel to that prevailing in the United States, where relatively little is done at the federal level (McKay, 1983). But while the United States has a long tradition of reliance on market mechanisms, this is not true for most of Western Europe. Strong industrial policies (e.g., social market, selective intervention, and occasionally even direct political control) are practiced in Western

*My thanks go to the Bowman Residence whose peace, quiet, and general support provided an extremely favorable environment for the rapid completion of this essay. I also want to acknowledge the inspiration of Christian Götz, reflected in especially subsections 2 and 3 of part II. Space limitations prevented me from discussion in greater depth the industrial policies of the four major EC nations: Great Britain, France, West Germany, and Italy.

27

European countries by the respective national governments. There is only a limited counterpart to this in the policies implemented in the United States at the state level. In any case, a policy that would correspond to the largely interventionist milieu of the EC member states has not been developed at the Community level.

There are various reasons for this situation. Part of the answer lies in the absence of a constitutional foundation for such a policy. More important is the lack of political will to strengthen European Community institutions, to think in Community rather than national terms. To a large degree this is due, at least for our problem areas, to important differences in industrial structures among the member nations as much as to differences in ideological habits and traditions. Divergent and occasionally mutually exclusive analyses and prescriptions regarding industrial problems often reflect a nationalistic bias and do not facilitate workable solutions to these problems. There is also the question of insufficient funds, particularly at a time of frequent budget crises. Before analyzing the main problems that have impeded a stronger Community approach, this essay will explore the different phases of EC thinking and practice with regard to industrial policy.

In discussing the EC approach, four phases from 1958 to the mid-1980s can be distinguished. The first phase was marked by the belief that competition in the newly integrated market (protected by the new external tariff) would by itself produce appropriate industrial structures with regard to size, increased efficiencies of scale, greater expenditure for R&D, profitability, market position, and the like. Before even the last customs tariffs on intra-Community trade of industrial products were abolished in 1968, this theory had been replaced by another one, that appropriate industrial structures of European dimensions would only come into being if they were actively promoted by the Community. By the mid-1970s, this phase in turn came to an end, partly because there was insufficient will to translate the belief characteristic of this phase into policy, partly because the faith in the superior efficiency of large oligopolies itself came into question. In the third phase, during the late 1970s, the Community became active in the field of industrial policy, but in a more defensive way—to attend to declining sectors that were threatened in their survival. In the most recent phase (since the early 1980s), the Community has taken more serious steps to promote the growth of competitive high-tech industries, at the same time that it tried to stabilize and to limit the scope of measures taken in favor of industrial sectors in difficulty.

Structural Change Through
Integration and Competition

When the Treaty of Rome was prepared, industrial policy
was not foremost in the minds of the Community's found-
ers. The treaty does not even provide a specific legal
basis for industrial policymaking, unlike the treaty
which set up the European Coal and Steel Community some
eight years earlier; however, the latter treaty was more
specific in every way. Nor was this lack of an industrial policy provision an accident. Such a policy simply was not thought to be necessary except for a brief
time during which the French government argued for
transposing its kind of planning to the European level,
without however being able to transfer new powers to
the EEC (Shonfield, 1963, pp. 146-147).
    The basic idea prevailing at that time was that the
reduction of impediments to intra-Community trade would
open up a new and large market for European producers.
Outsiders would be kept away by the Common External
Tariff. A large market, comparable in size to that of
the United States, would by itself lead to the modernization of industrial structures. The main thing that
needed to be safeguarded was the fairness of the competition among firms and, indirectly, among countries. No
firm should gain an undue advantage because of the support it might enjoy on its home front. Thus, it was
thought that the Community should limit its efforts to
guaranteeing market competition itself by checking the
absence of interventions that would have distorted that
competition; verifying the absence of market power; and
ensuring the progressive harmonization of business conditions, tax laws, disclosure requirements, labor prac-
tices, and the like throughout the countries of the
Community. The market would do the rest.

Seeking to Build European Champions

Several developments made it clear early on that the
market acting alone was not fulfilling these expecta-
tions. An unexpected result of the unified European
market was the installment of large U.S. corporations
seeking to take advantage of the new trading area while
at the same time overcoming the problem of the common
external tariff. This reduced the growth potential for
European firms considerably. One possible response to
this was to control U.S. investments in the Community
and, in fact, this is just what the French government
proposed to do (Calleo and Rowland, 1973; Vernon, 1974).
However, France could not secure a commitment from the
other EC members that they would not undercut the French
position by offering better terms to foreign investors.
This was an early manifestation of the "American challenge."

In the 1960s, it was widely thought (particularly in official circles) that greater size (oligopoly, essentially), was identical with greater efficiency, more rapid technological progress, and the like. In the mid-1960s, many member countries passed legislation to facilitate mergers, take-overs, and cooperation arrangements. But the member states promoted mergers only among "national" firms (not necessarily--in fact, not usually--public sector firms). These were used increasingly "in an effort to solve specific problems as if they were agencies of the state" (Vernon, 1974, p. 3). If governments sometimes encouraged these firms to also reach out, to set up subsidiaries, or even to negotiate cooperative ventures with firms of a different nationality, they did not tolerate schemes that would have placed the national identity of such firms in jeopardy (Vernon, 1974, p. 22). European corporate partnerships were difficult and, in fact, proved unstable in most cases.

This practice of promoting national champions worked against the economic integration (and the political spillover effects supposed to result therefrom) that the Community was meant to achieve. It pitted nation-states against each other. National champions also undermined the practice of the integrated market. Besides, they did not seem an appropriate response to policymakers who believed in the superior virtues of great size: even national champions merging several national firms could not stand up to the dimensions of the giant U.S. corporations. Thus, the response seemed divisive, nationalistic, provincial, and ineffective to the promoters of the European Community interest.

One of the early manifestations of a Community response is in a 1965 memo from Robert Toulemon to EEC Commissioner Guido Colonna di Paliano in which he proposed both control of U.S. investments and the promotion of corporate mergers. By 1966 a first medium-term program for economic policy had been worked out by the Commission; it was approved by the Council in early 1967. The program provided for the usual measures of harmonization, but also for the promotion of mergers (by removing legal obstacles on the part of member states) and sectoral policies for growing and declining sectors (Europäische Gemeinschaften, 1967). It was the first time that industrial policy goals were officially formulated within the Community.

The Commission put forth similar proposals in 1967 and 1969 which were ratified by the Council; they were also fairly specific on financial questions. Community finance would be provided only if firms could not handle structural adaptation out of their own funds. This assistance would be given only to profitable ventures, only to a few key industries occupying a strategic position for future technological progress. All assistance

would be limited in time, be degressive, and at least
partly refundable (Europäische Gemeinschaften, 1969).
All this meant that the Community organs were limiting
the scope of those articles of the EEC Treaty (especially articles 85 and 86) designed to secure competition
by preventing the build-up of dominant market positions.

The memos discussed thus far were never put into
practice; they did not get beyond the stage of discussions within the EC structure. In 1970 a more important
step was undertaken when the Commission submitted its
memorandum on industrial policy in the Community. The
Commission presented a common industrial policy as the
completion of the Common Market and again submitted very
specific measures. In particular, it proposed the harmonization of legal frameworks and the restructuring of
industrial firms. This was fleshed out by proposals to
sign development agreements to promote cooperation among
firms of different nationalities and to coordinate the
decline of traditional sectors.

The submission of the memorandum to the Council led
to intense controversy among member states. The Commission responded by modifying its original proposal.
In May 1973, it submitted a communication to the Council (EC Bulletin) in which it proposed additional powers for the Community in the area of industrial policy,
including powers to promote harmonization with regard
to legal conditions and mergers, financial powers, and
the power to lay down sectoral policies. The communication included first guidelines for the harmonization of
European corporate law and the model of a European corporation to be chartered directly under the authority
of the Community. It also set up a mechanism for the
provision of risk capital by the Community, and a European version of planning agreements to be funded with
EEC money.

But this time the Commission's proposals on industrial policy were already condemned by and large. The
Council now more or less ignored them. The main reason
for this was the impossibility of securing agreement
among member countries. Because of the Luxembourg com-
promise of 1966 which guaranteed that all important matters must be decided in the Council by a unanimous vote,
a majority decision was a constitutional but not a practical possibility. France was in favor of much of the
industrial policy program but objected to the transfer
of effective powers to the Community. West Germany was
prepared to discuss a general framework for industrial
policy but not sectoral plans or interventions that
would have been incompatible with market principles.
With the two major powers in conflict (the game was
complicated by others, at the end especially by British
objections to potential increases of the Community budget), all that came of nearly ten years of efforts was
the setting up of a marriage bureau for small and

medium-sized firms that were willing to cooperate.
Otherwise, the years of intensive discussion and conflict over industrial policy were followed by a period
of benign neglect. The Community returned to the subject after several years under very different conditions.
The last boom of the long period of postwar growth had
been replaced by a generalized crisis. In this crisis
many of Europe's industries suffered intensely. This
initiated a new round of Community efforts to work out
an industrial policy.

Attempting the Rescue of Crisis Sectors

From the mid-1970s onward, economic crisis was manifest
in EC countries. There were signs of it earlier: the
crisis of the international monetary system, the build-
up of inflationary tensions, and the fall in profit
rates (Lesourne, 1985, pp. 23-24; McCracken Report, 1977).
were phenomena that developed in the early 1970s, sometimes even in the late 1960s. Added to this was the
oil crisis and (partly as a result) the deepened crisis
of Keynesian economics, indeed of the social-democratic
consensus as a whole. Economic policy approaches proposed by European parties showed increasing discontinu-
ity, particularly in France and Britain (Lauber, 1983a).
Despite this crisis, wage levels in the Community generally kept increasing at first, with only a small setback
in 1976 (Eurostadt Review, 1981, p. 148). As a greater
share of value added was absorbed by labor costs, investment took a back seat. Stagnation of the world market
and increased competition from abroad reduced Western
Europe's exports to that market significantly. Partly
this was due to the rise of new industrial countries in
the semiperiphery (as in the case of textiles), partly
to the breakthrough of Japanese industry during this
time period. While the share of Japanese products going
to the U.S. market diminished from 1970 to 1980, the
share that went to the EC market increased dramatically
(Eurostadt Review, 1981, pp. 235, 239). Demographic
stagnation and the attained level of affluence also put
an end to traditional forms of infrastructure growth,
something that further reduced demand. All this led to
large unused capacities in industry and to considerable
job losses in sectors that from slow decline had now
moved to a phase of open crisis.
     Governmental responses varied according to coun-
tries and sectors. Overall there was a marked increase
in subsidies in order to stave off bankruptcies and
maintain employment, or at least to limit unemployment
to acceptable levels. Several countries resorted uni-
laterally to regulating trade in certain products by
means of voluntary agreements that limited imports or
by granting special conditions for export financing.
But, depending on such facts as the age of the capital

structure, the trade balance for certain products, or
(to a lesser degree) programmatic commitments, government responses varied widely. Again, Community integration was in jeopardy as national governments (even when
they did not diverge) tried to create special conditions for their "own" industry in order to help it
through the crisis. This problem was enhanced by the
fact that intra-Community trade also became more competitive. In particular, West German firms displaced
other European (especially French) producers from EC
markets, compensating their own declining performance
on the world market (which other European countries, as
a result, had to confront in an even more intense fashion (Lesourne, 1985, pp. 26-27). In this context,
there were several efforts by Community organs to secure
a common approach to the crisis and to prevent a regression of Community integration.

Steel.[2] The strongest action was taken in the steel sector. This is not surprising since the ECSC Treaty provides expressly for crisis mechanisms in the form of
minimum prices, import limitations, even quotas to be
apportioned among producers. Also, there is a clear
delegation of powers to the High Authority (powers which,
after the fusion of ECSC, Euratom, and EEC, were trans-
ferred to the European Commission).
    The European steel industry had been slow to moder-
nize before the recession. Import penetration steadily
increased already before the mid-1970s. All governments
intervened fairly heavily, despite substantial differences in doctrine. Subsidy levels were at comparable
levels in Germany and France, somewhat higher in Britain
and Italy. In all countries they rose after 1975.
Italy had the most modern installations by that date.
Britain had ambitious plans for modernization and expansion of British Steel Corporation (founded in 1968), but
these plans were not launched until 1975. Since the recession was already drastically restricting the market,
those modernization plans were cancelled, and the British steel sector was most severely affected by restric-
tive measures. In France, the state intervened in 1979
by a quasinationalization to save the steel industry
from bankruptcy. In Germany, governmental policy was
more interventionist in this sector than in many others
(Shepherd, 1984). In all countries employment in the
steel sector declined--34.9 percent for the EC overall
in the years 1974 to 1982. Figures were above average
for France (40 percent) and particularly for Britain
(60 percent) (deLettenhove, 1984).[3]
    The rescue efforts of the European Commission were
guided by Etienne Davignon. At first, the Commission
negotiated quotas among firms on a voluntary basis
(Eurofer cartel) and issued a code of conduct for national subsidies to the steel industry. This code

provided that subsidies should favor new investment or
the reduction of capacities and should not cover current deficits; it was renewed in 1980. In 1977 the
Commission also set minimum prices for certain steel
products and imposed tariffs on imports. As the situation deteriorated further, the Commission declared
that a situation of manifest crisis existed and imposed
the supervised cartel provided for in the ECSC Treaty.
This cartel was extended in subsequent years. There
were some problems, particularly with securing the
agreement of the Italian delegation. (Italy had the
newest production facilities and therefore most strongly resisted production quotas and especially reductions
of capacity.) (Götz, 1984, pp. 208-209).

The cartel and the subsidy code were not fully respected. Governments increased subsidies considerably
in 1981. Brussels authorities were not even notified
of some subsidies. Minimum prices were violated. Ex-
cess capacities were often not liquidated but only moth-
balled for later use. Even so, the cartel and the regulations that attended it amounted clearly to industrial
policy on the part of the Community. As things stood
early in 1985, subsidies were supposed to be eliminated
by the end of that year. It remains to be seen whether
that commitment will be respected.

Some Commission members (in particular Davignon
himself) hoped to extend the idea of a crisis cartel to
other areas as well. In 1977, the London summit meeting asked the European Commission to study sectoral
measures. The Commission responded the same year by
proposing a five-year program for industrial policy
which included immediate measures in favor of textiles
and shipbuilding, sectors that were to be treated similarly to steel. The proposal also provided for Community funding in such areas as energy, aerospace, and
electronics.

Textiles. The textile sector was to become the testing
ground for these initiatives. This sector had been in
difficulty for some time, with marked job losses throughout the Community. Between 1970 and 1978, the share of
imports in total consumption had almost doubled for
Britain, France, and Germany; the share of production
going to exports had increased at a much slower rate
(Jacquemin, 1984, pp. 140-141). Differences among the
major European countries were quite important. The
German textile industry had specialized early on in the
1960s; it was quite successful and made Germany the
world's largest textile exporter. The Italian industry
specialized in the 1970s, shifting over to a strongly
deconcentrated production structure in an attempt to
evade taxes, social security payments, and unionization.
It, too, was highly successful. The French industry
had long been backward and had undergone significant

mergers in the 1970s, with rationalization coming only late in that decade. The British textile industry, the most concentrated among the large industrial countries, suffered significant setbacks in the 1970s when its mass market strategy failed. The British industry was also one of the most protected in the EC. Specialization came only in the 1980s (Jacquemin, 1984, pp. 193-198).

The European textile industry as a whole suffered particularly from cheap exports by developing countries. A first regulation of imports took place within GATT as early as 1961. After the United States limited its imports from Southeast Asian countries in 1971 by bilateral negotiations, the Multifiber Arrangement (MFA) was signed in 1974 with EC participation to set up a framework for future trade, providing an exemption from GATT regulations. While imports to the United States were stabilized, they surged at first for the European Community (Farrands, 1979, p. 26). In 1976 France proposed a crisis cartel for man-made fibers, analagous to the regulation provided for steel (capacity reductions, market shares, minimum prices). The proposal was opposed by Italy and Ireland (countries that had just built up their own industries), and also by Germany. Finally, the major textile firms themselves proposed a cartel to the Commission, and Davignon persuaded the most reluctant Italian delegation not to further resist such a solution. The envisioned crisis cartel contained quotas for capacities, production, and distribution and planned a 15 percent capacity reduction.

This solution was arrived at without the agreement of the Council and in violation of article 85 of the EEC Treaty. But when, in July 1978, the eleven textile firms applied formally for a registration of this cartel by the Commission, there was a strong protest from German economics minister Lambsdorff, despite the fact that the German delegation to the Council had previously given its assent. He also persuaded French economics minister Monory to support this position. As a result, the Commission rejected the registration of the cartel on the grounds that it violated the Treaty of Rome. However, it did not at first take any sanctions against the eleven firms concerned (Curzon-Price, 1981, pp. 105-110; Götz, 1984, pp. 217-224).

With this step, a major development of the EC powers was effectively blocked. There were other measures taken in favor of the textile sector but they were largely restricted to stricter import quotas. Protectionism seemed to become the major way in which the Community could become active in industrial matters, except of course in the area of steel. This pattern was confirmed by developments regarding other crisis sectors. In 1977, the European Commission proposed to reduce shipbuilding capacity by 45 percent. This was rejected

by the Council. As a result, the Commission limited
itself to proposing a ceiling on subsidies amounting to
30 percent of production costs--not a drastic measure
by any means. It also tried to exert pressure on Japan.
In neither area did it have much success (Götz, 1984,
pp. 211-217).

Automobiles. In other areas, the European Community
played an even lesser role. The automobile industry is
a case in point. Between 1960 and 1980, the automobile
industry evolved to the disadvantage of the major EC
countries. While imports rose sharply, exports stagnated. The evolution was particularly dramatic in
Great Britain and Italy, less so in France and Germany.
In any case, there was no common approach.

Since World War II, the European governments had
viewed the automobile industry as an instrument to improve the balance of payments, to develop backward regions, and to stabilize the economy. Strong relationships between national governments and their respective
car makers built up, even in the case of West Germany.
Major producers in France (Renault), Britain (BL, later
also Rolls Royce), and Italy (Alfa-Romeo) were in the
public sector. In Germany this applied to VW (owned by
the Federal Republic and by Lower Saxony, with each
holding 20 percent of the capital) (Wells, 1974).

European integration and the end of protection by
national tariffs was soon followed by the first appearance of Japanese cars on European markets. This led to
strong policies of national protection by non-tariff
barriers. In 1973, Italy already had an import quota
of 1,000 Japanese cars (Wells, 1974, p. 243). Great
Britain negotiated voluntary export restraints (VER)
with Japan in 1976. France limited its imports uni-
laterally in 1977 to 3 percent of the domestic market.
Germany followed suit with a VER in 1981, but only after
the United States had forced VER on Japanese car makers.
A common approach was further undercut by the lack of
agreement on the question of foreign investment. While
France and Italy allowed virtually no foreign investment, Britain made efforts to attract a Japanese firm
(Nissan) in order to set up operations there (Shepherd,
1984, pp. 201-202). Thus, there is a key industry with
a record of large-scale public intervention by national
governments but with virtually no agreement on a Community approach. There is only a modest chance that
this state of affairs will change in the late 1980s with
the introduction of Community approval of vehicles imported from outside the Community (Defreigne, 1984, p.
373).

Concentrating on Positive Adjustment?

While the EC thus made efforts to come up with a common
policy at least in some crisis sectors (efforts that
soon proved unsuccessful), a common industrial policy
for growth sectors remained even more out of its reach.
In 1970, growth sectors were clearly included in the
abortive Commission memorandum on industrial policy
described above. In 1973 an active industrial policy
recommended by Altieri Spinelli was considered for problem and growth sectors. The Commission reiterated this
view in 1977. But absorbed as the Commission was by
this time with the task of rescuing crisis sectors, its
concern with growth sectors led to almost no action at
all. A few small research programs for electronics were
adopted in the second half of the 1970s, often with long
delays (Götz, 1984, pp. 228-229). It must, of course,
be added that national considerations are very strong
in many advanced technology sectors, for reasons of defense (nuclear, aerospace), technological leadership,
national independence, and prestige. For that reason
as well, Community initiatives in this area were bound
to meet with strong national resistance.

However, there were signs of a possible change in
the early 1980s. First of all, the high point of intervention by the national governments of member countries
in favor of declining sectors was passed during this
time and the limits of such an approach became more and
more apparent. In Great Britain, the election of
Margaret Thatcher as Prime Minister was an important
milestone, although subsidies could not be cut as quickly as one might have expected (e.g., in the case of British Steel Corporation; Grant, 1982, pp. 93-94); but as
shown earlier, they followed a declining trend since
the mid-1970s. In Germany, the reversal (in terms of
thinking, if not always in terms of practical politics)
came about under the Social Democrats; the major step
was the governmental crisis of 1982 and the access to
power of the Christian Democrats after the Liberals'
policy shift. In France, the Socialists seemed to go
against the trend at first; however, they fell in line
at least partially in 1983-84. A different policy began to take shape in those countries and in the OECD
generally; the emphasis shifted to "positive adjustment,"
to efforts to build up competitive industries in growth
sectors rather than trying to save jobs in declining
sectors at ever-increasing costs and without the hope
of returning those sectors to their former importance
or profitability. The Japanese "MITI-approach" (trying
to pick strategic, capital- and knowledge-intensive industries with high value added and rapidly growing markets) came to be regarded as the most promising policy
for Europe as well. It was not exactly a new idea by
this time, but it was clearly gaining ground.

In 1980, the European Commission passed some measures that in due course should limit national aid to
problem sectors. One was the model code for national
subsidies to the steel industry (a sector that absorbed
a large share of all public subsidies). This code
placed a curb on subsidies destined simply to cover
current losses and permitted future subsidies only for
new investment. Even those subsidies had to be limited
in time and had to follow a schedule that specified the
year by which they were to be terminated. Also in 1980,
in another move, the Commission issued a guideline re-
quiring public sector firms to lay open the transfer
payments they received from their governments. This
guideline was challenged by Great Britain, France, and
Italy before the European Court of Justice. However,
the Court ruled in 1982 in favor of the Commission,
which can now exert pressure on governments and make
their transfers to public sector firms more difficult
(EC Bulletin, 1982, p. 31).

More important perhaps for the policy of positive
adjustment, the Commission again in 1980 started the
European Strategic Program for Research in Information
Technology (ESPRIT) which for years met with resistance
in the Council. Its goal was to build up a strong European electronics industry by putting an end to the
squabbling between member states and their firms (often
national champions) and to mark a breakthrough that
might establish the European electronics industry on
the international scene. At stake were not only computers in the narrow sense, but the whole range of information technology: from telecommunications and
broadcasting to consumer electronics, numerical command
machines, and the like--a good part of the "third" industrial revolution.

The European computer market had fallen to U.S.
firms in the 1960s, due primarily to the commercial
(and only later to the technological) superiority of
those firms, in particular IBM (Jéquier, 1974, p. 199).
In part, U.S. firms conquered market shares through
predatory pricing policies in Europe's mostly unprotect-
ed markets. This illustrated the extent to which the
reduction of the Common External Tariff by the Kennedy
Round had left European spearhead industries without
protection (Defreigne, 1984, p. 368; Shepherd, 1984, p.
208). It was difficult to mount a counterattack once
the fort was already half conquered. Industrial success often depends on the past record of accumulation
with regard to capital, technology, and expertise
(Jacquemin, 1984, p. 2). By the late 1960s, this process of accumulation already favored non-European firms,
especially those of the United States, and it was difficult to dislodge them from their positions by belated
national (and possibly quite inappropriate) policies.

A response took shape in the 1960s on the national
level among three of the four larger members of the current Community. Great Britain (with ICL) and France
(with CII and Bull) decided to do battle in defense of
the national champions they now fostered; Germany followed suit a few years later with Siemens. Italy, by
contrast, acted more like a small country and did not
adopt a national champion policy. These three countries
promoted a series of mergers among their national firms
in order to create champions large enough to possess
what was widely considered a desirable stature (Jéquier,
1974, pp. 215-216). Of course, these mergers could not
resolve the problem of insufficient national markets.[4]
Considerable funds were thus spent on financial assistance. Even West Germany spent $1.6 billion between
1967 and 1982, mostly on Siemens, in the hope that this
firm would become a competitor for IBM--a hope that
never came close to being fulfilled (English, 1984).
The European Community gave the following figures for
subsidies to the electronics industry in the three countries listed for 1976-1979: $800 million in Germany,
$500-$600 million in France, and over $800 million in
Great Britain (Thorn, 1984, p. 4). Despite these
amounts, the three countries achieved only modest results, their respective national champions could secure
about half ot their national markets in the early 1980s.
Outside of their home territories, they were in a rather
hopeless position (English, 1984, p. 230).

The history of transnational cooperation among
European firms is not a very happy one. This started
quite early with Bull's joining up with General Electric
(the U.S. corporation) and Honeywell between 1964 and
1970 (Jéquier, 1974, p. 215). In 1972 Philips (Netherlands), Siemens (West Germany), and CII (France) set up
a computer firm, UNIDATA. However, cooperation did not
last, partly because these firms were competing in
another area, i.e., telephone equipment. In 1975,
UNIDATA fell apart. The following year, CII merged with
Honeywell-Bull, which became the only large computer
firm in France besides IBM.

It took many years before another merger of a comparable size was attempted. In 1982 Thomson-Brandt
(France) and Grundig (West Germany) joined forces to
produce consumer electronics. The merger was stopped
by political resistance in Germany and a negative opinion of the German Cartel Commission in early 1983. The
Commission argued that the proposed merger would have a
negative impact on competition. The real reason for the
resistance lay elsewhere: Thomson had been nationalized
in early 1982 and, since it would have been the senior
partner in the merger, the possibility of French political choices affecting the German electronics industry
were opened. Rather than persist in its merger initiative (the cartel commission does not have final say in

this matter), Thomson turned to a less interesting and less compatible firm, AEG-Telefunken. Grundig oriented itself toward Philips (the Netherlands) which was not backed by a strong national government or a powerful country (English, 1984, pp. 267-268; Götz, 1984, pp.230-233). In 1982, ICL, Bull, and Siemens established a joint institute in Bavaria for research in advanced computer systems. The same year, Philips and Siemens announced plans for cooperation in long-lead research and development (English, 1984, p. 267).

For a long time, Community organs were slow in developing initiatives in this sector. In 1976, the European Commission first recommended standardization of equipment, uniform procurement policies, and Community support for research. The firm concentration issue was not even touched upon. Only in 1979 did the Council finally act upon this proposal and, even then, only in an extremely modest fashion, appropriating only one quarter of the amount recommended by the Commission three years earlier (Götz, 1984, pp. 228-230). In the early 1980s, however, more significant progress was made. In December 1982, the Council adopted several Commission proposals that aimed at promoting investment in strategic areas--energy, biotechnology, and information technology. In 1983, the Commission proposed expansion of direct Community lending for industrial development; this was quickly adopted by the Council. With the New Community Instrument (NCI), the EC serves as intermediary between international capital markets and EC firms. In 1982, total Community lending under the headings of the European Investment Bank, ECSC, Euratom, and the new NCI amounted to 5.25 billion ECUs; in 1983, NCI alone added another 3 billion ECUs (Wilkinson, 1984, pp. 67-69).

Finally, there is ESPRIT. The European Commission had worked on this program since 1980. National governments were reluctant to agree on a common policy and, as a result, the Council blocked the Commission initiative for several years. In February 1984 the Council adopted the ESPRIT program. It set the goal for the Community to conquer one third of the world market in information technology and provided to this effect 1.5 billion ECU to finance research and development from 1984 to 1988 by European electronics firms. Industry and other sources had to come up with a matching amount for this program to become operational (Wilkinson, 1984). The program was quite pervasive; thus, the Commission called upon machine tool manufacturers to submit joint proposals with electronics manufacturers for numerical command machines for funding under ESPRIT (English, 1984, p. 236. Twelve large firms, several firm groups, and hundreds of small and medium-sized firms started working together. In August 1984, 90 projects were ready for adoption. The twelve large firms cooperating under ESPRIT also worked on common standards and on uniform design beginning in 1985, with the intention of getting the Commission to adopt these standards for future public procurement (Defreigne, 1984, p. 372; English, 1984, p. 267; Thorn, 1984, p. 3). In February 1985, several European electronics producers also decided to achieve software compatibility as soon as possible. At last, there seems to be a large strategic sector--and one in which national ambitions had long prevented common undertakings--in which a Community approach seems to be forthcoming. If successful, this could set a precedent for other areas.

From the mid-1970s to 1983, the European Community was characterized by an emphasis on welfare at the expense of industrial renewal. There was a first increase in industrial investment (about 3.5 percent) in 1984; for 1985 a much larger increase is expected (Davignon, 1984). It is too early to say what the new phase that has just begun is likely to bring; but it seems possible that in the changed environment an affirmative industrial policy of the European Community might yet develop.

CONCLUSION

An overview of industrial policy at the Community level forces the conclusion that, with the exception of steel, Community policy is extremely fragile and exists only in rudimentary form. Several initiatives at strengthening it were defeated. Such a situation is surprising. After all, the large countries of the Community all practice strong industrial policies at home, although with considerable variations from country to country. Why did such a strongly interventionist milieu not lead to a stronger Community policy? And will the learning experience of the last 25 years contribute to changing the situation?

The explanations for this situation are to be found on several levels. First, industrial and demographic structures often vary greatly from country to country; this leads to conflicting interests. Second, conflicting ideologies (whether of nation-states or political parties) often oppose each other and frequently lead to paralysis. Third, there is real fear involved in giving up the familiar national units and staking the future on the success of a relatively recent artificial construct, i.e., the European Community. Fourth, there is the problem of resources and distribution: the Community's budget problems make it difficult to use sums that would be comparable to the expenditures made by the member states for their own policies to enhance a Community industrial policy. Finally, there is the constitutional problem: the powers delegated to Community organs in the area of industrial policy are so

modest as to permanently place any such policy in fundamental jeopardy.

Conflicting Interests

Different interests result from diverging demographic
and industrial structures. From 1970 to 1979 there was
relative stability in Great Britain and West Germany,
contrasting with a considerable increase (5-6 percent)
in France and Italy. This explains in part the different evolution of industrial employment in those countries (regression by over 10 percent in Great Britain
and West Germany, by only about 5 percent in France,
and a slight increase in Italy). The contrast is even
stronger between the EC and its main rivals: the United
States and Japan, where population strongly increased
over the same time period. It is interesting to note
that industrial employment as percent of total civilian
employment declined throughout the EC from a relatively
high level in 1970, a level that was considerably higher than that of the United States or Japan.
     The national structures of the four major Community
member states are sufficiently different to frequently
make for diverging interests among them. In the 1960s
and early 1970s, firm size was given great significance,
with oligopolies being viewed very widely as being superior in technological and commercial efficiency. There
were considerable variations in the geographic distribution of the largest firms in the Community. The same
is true of differences in capital intensity, the average
age of capital investment in given sectors, and profitability in different sectors. Differing levels of competitiveness (in West Germany, the share of competitive
industries is relatively large, while it is lowest in
Great Britain; Lesourne, 1984, p. 23) also lead to different trade balances for different sectors.
     British and French deficits on intra-Community
trade increased over the last decade while West Germany
increased its surplus (Lesourne, 1984, p. 27). This is
likely to lead to different approaches to protection of
the home market and to even more straightforward beggar-
thy-neighbor policies. Examples include the British invitation for U.S. and Japanese investments in automobile
and computer production at a time when other European
countries tried to reduce surplus capacity or unify policy; and competitive subsidization as it was practiced
for steel, textiles, and shipbuilding. Differences in
the ties between firms and their respective national
governments--often based on long-standing traditions--
also lead to conflicting situations. The 1980 guideline for public sector firms issued by the Commission
represents an effort to reduce one source of differences in this area.

Conflicting Ideologies

Conflicting ideologies certainly played an important
role at the Community level. Ideological traditions
vary by country, with West Germany usually taking the
free market/free trade position, France a more interventionist stance, and Great Britain a more protectionist one. Ideology also varies according to parties in
power. Here, the variations were particularly great in
France and Great Britain, to a lesser extent also in
West Germany. Some EC observers complain that ideological controversy at times dominates discussion at the expense of a more factual approach. Since 1983, however,
the situation has been relatively favorable in this respect, at least as far as the four major member states
are concerned.

Fear of Supranationality

More is at stake here than industrial policy alone. The
problem was aptly summed up in the early days of the
Community by de Gaulle: people are willing to die only
for their own country. The goal of the European Community is progressive integration--economic, but also
political. A recurrent fear is that, while it may be
possible to transfer constitutional powers to the EC,
loyalties are not as easily shifted. Another fear concerns the transfer of control over the fate of a national community to a little-known entity. What if the
Community organs should never enjoy widespread legitimacy among the populations of the member states? Or
worse, what if it should conduct an irresponsible policy? With such doubts (voiced particularly by French
leaders), it becomes problematic to turn over one's industry to the discretion of an international (or supranational) organization. To do so may even go against
the first duty of a nation-state which consists in pro-
tecting its own citizens--their welfare, their employment, their security, their life chances generally.
And, if the Community is to reorganize a whole industrial sector (or all of industry) in the light of the
larger Community interest, it will not always be able
to satisfy national aspirations. That is the logic of
a large market, of a Community interest different from
a national interest.
        Confronted with this problem, states repeatedly
shrunk back from turning over vital matters to Community
decisions. Even when they did, the unanimity rule sub-
stantially restricted the scope for "supranational" decision making. So far, there has been little spontane-
ous convergence among the member states. The enlarge-
ment of the Community makes such progress even more
difficult. Given the prevailing circumstances, the goal

of unification remains as remote today as it was two
decades ago.

Insufficient Resources

The EC budget allows for only about 1,500 ECUs to be
spent on industrial and related policies while the
nation-states expend 350,000 ECUs for this purpose.
Over 90 percent of the Community budget is spent on
agriculture through the CAP, a program the nation-states
have agreed to support. Given the repeated EC crises
over budgetary problems in recent years, new programs
will not be established easily. NCI and ESPRIT are
modest first steps. A further problem is the desire of
member states to get a fair return (juste retour) for
their budget contributions. This means that countries
should roughly get back what they paid in--an approach
that would reduce industrial policymaking to an exercise in pork-barrel politics and greatly hamper its economic efficiency (See B. Guy Peters, this volume).
Greater financial resources and more numerous programs
would make such side payments possible; but the industrial policy resulting from this would likely waste resources. On the other hand, the current lack of resources may prevent an industrial policy altogether. It
is a difficult dilemma.

Constitutional Problems

The problem of insufficient powers is a fundamental one;
it results from both the wording of the EEC Treaty and
subsequent practice. The drafters of the treaty were
guided by the idea that industrial regulation would assist in securing free competition (e.g., no dominant
market positions, no distortion of competition by national subsidies) of trade between member countries and
a strong common external tariff. An active industrial
policy was not planned and has no express basis in the
treaty.
　　This legal problem need not be insurmountable. The
Treaty of Rome represents a constitution that can evolve
over time. It even contains an article that expressly
permits constitutional evolution. Article 235 represents something like an "implied powers" formula:

> If a goal of the EEC can only be realized by an
> activity of the Community and if the Treaty does
> not expressly provide the necessary powers, then
> the Council may by unanimous decision, after hear-
> ing the Commission and the Assembly, lay down
> those powers by decree.

The possibility of expanding Community powers, then, is
clearly there. However, it is not an independent court
which decides such issues by a majority, but a political

body (the Council) in which every member state is represented, and the decision must be unanimous. This means that any member state can torpedo a policy that does not have a solid constitutional basis. This is what, in fact, has happened repeatedly, e.g., with the 1970 memorandum on industrial policy, and with the Davignon proposals concerning crisis cartels.

Another possible basis for industrial policy is contained in article 130 which sets down the rules for a European Investment Bank. This bank is supposed to promote the modernization of enterprises in cases where the member states are unable to do so individually, and generally to finance projects which, because of their nature or size, are beyond the financial means of individual member states. However, the European Investment Bank, since the mid-1970s, has been used primarily for regional development and energy projects (Götz, 1984, pp. 116-117). The European Social Fund and the European Fund for Regional Development yielded even fewer industrial policy applications.

Thus, the industrial policy of the Community rests on a basis which is fragile not only in political but also in legal terms. To some extent, the situation is comparable to that of the North Aemrican colonies under the Articles of Confederation before the interstate commerce clause was introduced by the new Constitution. In other respects, it resembles that of the United States before the acceptance of the New Deal (and the expansion of powers based on the interstate commerce clause) by the Supreme Court. However, there is no Supreme Court available to resolve the issue in Europe; the European Court of Justice lacks the necessary powers. As with the founding fathers in the days of the American Constitutional Convention, the real question may be whether the member states of the European Community, confronted with a world of intense international competition, will hang together or whether they will hang separately. It would be a poor consolation, in case the latter event should come to pass, that at least they would all hang from the same tree.

NOTES

1. Industrial policy is understood here as being concerned with industrial structures, not with regional development. The policy practiced in many states of the United States is often regional more than national industrial policy.

2. For this part of the subsection I owe substantial inspiration to Christian Götz, "Regimeverhandlungen in den Europäischen Gemeinschaften" (Salzburg: unpublished doctoral dissertation, 1984), pp. 106-111.

3. Percentage figures were calculated by Christian Götz.

4.   Individual European countries are unlikely to
represent more than about 5 percent of the world market
for computers, for example.
5.   For a summary of Western Europe's recovery,
see the bulletin Conjoncture (Paris: Paribas, February
1985), pp. 17-22.   On the whole subject of industrial
renewal in the Community, see Launching High-Technology
Business in Europe, and Industrial Innovation: A Guide
to Community Action, Services and Funding (both available from Brussels: Agence Europe/European Research Associates, 1983).

4
The Politics of Industrial Policy in the United States

B. Guy Peters

The title of this essay would have been met with blank
stares in the United States even five years ago. It is
indicative of the real or perceived changes in the economic position of this country that we have now begun
to think about deviating from a received wisdom (at
least a conventional wisdom) of nonintervention in the
economy other than through general, macro-level programs. At this time, a program of direct sectoral intervention by the federal government is being discussed
more seriously. Sectoral policies would not really be
as great a deviation as sometimes imagined; tariffs,
subsidies, loan guarantees, and other means have been
used, and at some points in our history used extensive-
ly, to promote or protect certain industries. The success of American agriculture on world markets is to no
small degree a function of a particular type of industrial policy. Even the railroads, which have been cited in television advertising as an example of the success of the free enterprise system, were spread across
the country with the assistance of government. What is
different now is that there is an attempt to develop a
more systematic approach to industrial policy directed
at restoring the place of the United States in the
world economy. Politically, words such as "comprehensive," "planned," and "integrated" have negative conno-
tations for the average American. Thus, the politics
of formulating any meaningful industrial policy within
the political and ideological context of the United
States--even if such a strategy were desirable--are extremely problematic.
   Not being an economist, I will tread lightly over
the subject of whether an industrial policy is indeed
desirable; a great deal of ink has been spread on that
subject already with few firm conclusions other than
that industrial policy is a growth industry for economists (Bluestone & Harrison, 1982; Lawrence, 1984; Reich
and Magaziner, 1982). Rather, this essay will be concerned with the <u>political</u> realities which may make a

comprehensive industrial policy at the federal level in
the United States infeasible even if it were to be considered economically desirable. It is argued that an
industrial policy developed by the federal government,
given its patterns of policymaking, might be worse than
nothing, since it would be expensive and unlikely to
produce any real benefits. Some of the significant
features of policymaking in the United States and the
difficulties that these present for imposing any coordinated and integrated policies will be discussed.
Some implicit if not explicit comparisons with other
industrial countries that have been more successful in
formulating and implementing such policies will be made.

THE SOURCE OF THE CONTROVERSY

Much of the seemingly increasing demand for an industrial policy arises from the perception that the United
States can no longer compete on world markets and that,
as a consequence, our country has become "deindustrial-
ized." There certainly has been economic growth during
the last decade, but this growth is largely in the service sectors of the economy; most basic manufacturing--
steel, other metals, automobiles, and even high technology manufacturing such as microchips--is now occurring
overseas. Government policies have had a great deal to
do with the success of some countries in "stealing" American jobs. The most common and over-used example is
the Ministry of International Trade and Industry (MITI)
in Japan which, through trade policy and careful management of financial resources, has been able to produce
what has been called the Japanese miracle. Although
apparently less omniscient than MITI, the governments
of many European countries have been criticized for using trade restrictions, finance, and dumping to promote
their own industries at the expense of American industry. On the other hand, the federal government in the
United States is seen as unwilling or unable to develop
effective trade policies which might counteract the actions taken by the foreign governments (U.S. House of
Representatives, 1977, pp. 72 ff.; 1978, pp. 88-89).
In fact, many traditional American economic policies
such as antitrust, free trade, and extensive regulatory
policies are perceived as reducing the competitiveness
of American commodities on world markets (for an obviously biased view, see American Iron and Steel Institute, 1981). Also, the financial system of the United
States has been cited as being particularly unhelpful
in maintaining or expanding the industrial base of the
country (Hatsopoulos, 1983; Zysman, 1983). There is
substantial disagreement on whether the deindustrialization phenomenon is more real than imagined; and, indeed,
what it means if it has occurred (Klein, 1983; Lawrence,
1984). However, as we are examining the development of

industrial policy from a political perspective, the appearance of the problem is sufficient to have it placed on the policymaking agenda (Kingdon, 1984). The appearance of a problem in American industry is very real, with both business and labor leaders outdoing each other in their attempts to draw attention to the problem.

A large number of the pressures on the American economy arise from the increasing importance of the international economy to domestic economy of the United States. The first oil crisis brought the fact of this interdependence home to the population in a rather dramatic way; but, if anything, international trade has increased as a proportion of the total United States economy since that time. By 1984, 75 percent of American industry was subject to international competition (U.S. House of Representatives, 1984). Compared to our trading partners, the American economy is still quite autonomous; but, compared to our previous experiences, international economics now has a significant impact on domestic economic conditions. Again, politically, it is the international dimension of the problems that are most often cited as amenable to rapid correction by government. Certainly, business leaders complain about high union wages and, to some degree, about the costs of government regulations; and labor leaders complain about the tendency of American businesses to take profits rather than reinvest in new plants. What they can agree on is that they face stiff and, to them, unfair competition from foreign producers. Many further agree that the government can act to ameliorate the problems created by increased foreign competition. Thus, the policymaking process has tended to be crowded with proposals to create barriers to international trade to correct industrial problems, while the range of tools available in the industrial policy toolkit is actually much greater.

POLICY OPTIONS FOR THE UNITED STATES

The term "industrial policy" has come to mean any number of things depending upon who is describing it and in what context. The question of whether the United States should adopt an industrial policy, therefore, depends upon the definition of the term being used. In some ways, there is already an industrial policy in place, even at the level of the federal government. When the activities of state and local governments are considered, the problem is not the absence of an industrial policy but the presence of too many policies which frequently work to counteract each other. As noted, there is a tendency to think of industrial policy only as alleviating the current problems of industries through the manipulation of international trade, but that is perhaps the most limited of the opportunities available to government. Choosing an industrial policy involves choices along several dimensions.

Sector or General Policies?

The first major choice which must be made is whether the "industrial policy" to be adopted will be industry specific or not. The traditional preference in economic policy in the United States has been for policies that are neutral among industries and tend to encourage all forms of business activities. A number of such policies are already in place, including the general "supply side" ideas of the Reagan administration and the associated reductions in personal and corporate income taxation (Bostworth, 1984). Other such activities include federal loans for small businesses (if not terminated in the FY 1986 budget), insurance for the banking systems, numerous depreciation and research and development provisions in the tax code, and "buy American" programs for governmental procurement. The economic logic of such general programs is that government is not capable of picking which industries are worthy and needful of specific supports and, therefore, policies are likely to be costly (in terms of real and opportunity costs) if it intervenes more directly. Therefore, providing a positive business climate and helping all industries equally is the best strategy. The political logic of this approach is that the federal government does not like to be seen as differentially rewarding (and by inference differentially disadvantaging) any specific industries or regions. Programs which spread their benefits equally and indirectly are much more acceptable to most American politicians.

There are, of course, strong and increasing pressures for more industry-specific programs. These programs are of two types. Certainly the most pressure in the Rust Belt is to bail out declining industries, especially heavy industry. This is "lemon socialism" at its best, or worst (McKay, 1983). This bail-out strategy is justified in terms of maintaining employment for large numbers of workers, many of whom, because of age and lack of formal education, are not capable of adjusting to structural change and finding new employment in jobs paying anything close to their wage levels in the steel or automobile industries. One estimate is that auto workers who do find jobs after being laid off have had to accept reductions of 30 percent in their previous wages and with many fewer fringe benefits (Bluestone, 1985). Bail-outs of heavy industry are further justified in terms of national security and the need to have a viable primary metals industry. The only other economic justification has been that these are "linkage" industries which provide inputs into a number of other industries and, therefore, should be maintained as an infrastructure for the rest of American industry. Clearly, however, the principal justification for such a policy would be to function as a form of disguised welfare or unemployment benefit for workers in industries that are no longer competitive internationally. This is a persuasive political argument in the steel valleys, but much less so elsewhere. Such a program would, however, conform to the conventional political formula of concentrated benefits and dispersed costs that Wilson (1980) has argued typifies much of American public policy.

A variation of the sectoral industrial policy to shelter declining industries is to use the tax and tariff system of the United States to shelter certain industries from international competition. One strategy in particular has been advocated which would attempt to match foreign subsidies for exports with our own industrial subsidies for the same products. In other words, if a country or group of countries decides to subsidize the price of steel in order to gain a larger market share in the United States, the American government should respond with a subsidy to the industry so that it can sell steel at the same price in the domestic market. The alternative approach to such subsidies is, of course, simply to send a polite note of appreciation to any country willing to sell goods to us a below the cost of production. That could well be the response of the consumer, but it would not be the response of the worker or managers of the steel industry. Given that we know that consumers tend not to be very well organized and that the argument of national interest provokes an immediate response in the American breast, political realities may make some response to international competition by subsidies or tariffs or the enforcement of anti-dumping legislation quite likely (American Iron and Steel Institute, 1983).

Another problem with any strategy of maintaining traditional, heavy industry is that attempts to maintain high prices for steel and automobiles may mean that workers with very low wages are being asked indirectly to subsidize the wages of workers who make much higher wages, and hence a very large equity problem is built into any attempt to prop up the declining industries (Lawrence, 1985). If the wage subsidies are more direct than through prices, the inequities become even greater and more visible. The service workers are, as a whole, less well-organized than industrial workers and may be less able to defend their interest through the political process.

The alternative type of industry-specific industrial policy would attempt to pick winners rather than bail out losers. Such a strategy would not prop up the industries of the past but would try to find the industries of the future. During the last days of the Carter administration, some ideas about "reconstruction finance" surfaced, with the prospect of providing venture capital for new and/or expanding industries. The international evidence for the success of such programs is spotty at best. There is some evidence of success in Japan and some more modest successes in some of the Western European countries (Hills, 1983; Johnson, 1982; Katzenstein, 1984). Even for Japan, however, there are those who argue that the successes are a function of the internal dynamics of Japanese industry, especially the willingness to cross-subsidize products and impose high internal prices in order to have lower prices in the international market, rather than the omniscience of MITI or the rest of the Japanese government. There are, in fact, some accounts of the same type of intrabureaucratic bargaining and warfare in Japan that have been cited as one of the weaknesses of American policy-making. Thus, relying on a strategy of picking winners, while seemingly quite rational and forward-looking, has little empirical support; it involves a number of assumptions about the abilities of economic and industrial planners to influence public policy. They would probably also require a very different type of industrial and economic/political structure than exists within the United States.

Newer industries have less of a political base than older declining industries. Steel, automobiles, and other heavy industry have had decades to establish their political ties with Congress and have obvious institutional "targets" within government where they can focus their lobbying activities. Newer industries often do not have even an established location and tend to employ fewer workers than older heavy industry, and hence are not likely to be able to wield the type of political clout of those older industries (Etzioni, 1983). Conservative advocates of the free market have had similar fears about the impact of industrial policies on economic growth (Badaracco & Yoffie, 1983). From a more objective stance, Walters (1984) has summarized this argument as follows:

> Given the open, pluralistic structure of the American political system, an industrial policy would favor large, regionally concentrated, traditional manufacturing industries employing large labor forces that can mobilize effective political demand. Over the long run, industrial policy would more likely result in retardation of structural adjustment in the American economy on behalf of declining industries than in the acceleration of structural change toward sunrise industries with the greatest prospects of growth (p. 37).

One additional problem with the strategy of picking winners is that it does little or nothing for the workers and regions that have been impacted by structural change. If indeed one of the pressing needs for an industrial policy is to find something meaningful to do for laid-off steel workers, auto workers, and the like, then a strategy assisting high-technology industries of the future may do little to return those workers to a productive economic life. Attempts to use similar strategies in the Research Triangle in North Carolina as a means of helping extremely poor workers or unemployed in that region appear to have had little success; yuppies have moved into that one region of North Carolina but the rest of the state has been affected only slightly. Displaced workers may get jobs in service industries which support the high-tech industries, but almost certainly at wages far below their previous wages. It is questionable whether even agressive labor market policies such as those developed in Sweden for dealing with economic dislocations resulting from international competition would be very successful for American workers (Lindbeck, 1976). Thus, a strategy for picking winners may simply provide funds for gambles on the industrial future without addressing many of the political demands which led to the interest in the strategy in the first place.

The defense industry, of course, has had a sectoral industrial policy benefiting it for a number of years. Here the claim of national interest is especially strong, and there is a felt need to have a large and technologically advanced weapons industry. This could hardly be counted as a coherent industrial policy, however, except to the extent of the extremely close linkages between the Department of Defense and defense contractors. This is especially true of the "Big Eight" contractors which account for almost one-third of all defense contracts and a similar proportion of the 2.8 million jobs created by defense contracting (Council on Economic Priorities, 1981). One can make the argument that the concentration on defense and space technologies actually has a negative impact on industrial performance in the United States (McKay, 1983). Although total research and development expenditures are high in the United States, a very large proportion is directed toward defense and space, leaving relatively little for other industrial purposes. There have been spin-offs from defense and space technology-- Teflon pans and Teflon presidencies indicate the real and rhetorical benefits--but certainly less has been realized than might be expected from an R&D strategy more directly oriented toward industrial and economic growth in general. Again, given the political realities, both domestic and international, such high levels of defense expenditures and defense research and development funds are likely to persist. Further, it may be difficult to generate significant amounts of federal research money for other than defense; as the fiscal screws tighten on the federal budget, one of the earliest candidates for termination has been basic research even in the natural sciences and engineering. Further, there is some evidence to indicate that a directly targeted policy might not be as effective as a semi-targeted policy of providing funds for basic research (Nelson and Langlois, 1983).

Regional Targeting

As well as deciding whether an industrial policy should be industry specific or not, a second decision must be made about the intended geographical effects of the policy. Of course, to the extent that certain industries are concentrated geographically, e.g., automobiles and steel, the two decisions may be the same. However, much of the existing industrial policy in the United States is directed more toward regions than industries. Few of these policies are managed by the federal government; most are operated by state and local governments, with their own regions being the intended beneficiaries. In fact, rather than not having an industrial policy, it could be argued that the United States suffers from too many industrial policies, with each of the states and most large cities actively pursuing industries through a hugh variety of locational incentives (Hansen, 1984; Jacobs, 1980).

In principle, there is little wrong with industrial and economic growth policies managed by subnational governments. Given that these governments will tend to know their own particular needs and circumstances better than would a central government, there is some logical justification for such decentralized policymaking. However, in practice, the ability of all state and local governments, regardless of their relative economic conditions, to manage such programs means that, rather than producing positive incentives for firms to locate in one place or another, the policies amount to subsidies to the firms with little or no competitive advantage among different states. Industrial policy, therefore, becomes an exercise in "beggar they neighbor" with little added to the relative attractiveness of one locality over another. Interestingly, however, if that is the case, then policies intended to be regionally selective may actually function as a general policy which will encourage businesses regardless of where they may attempt to locate.

Not only is the logic of competitive industrial policies somewhat flawed, but the instruments which most state and local governments attempt to manipulate tend to be suboptimal as well. Most states and localities

utilize tax forgiveness and reductions as the principal
means to induce industries to locate within their borders. Interestingly, even for states with established
industrial bases, these preferences tend to be given to
new industries rather than to existing firms--even those
faced with competitive problems. Thus, although basic
steel and other primary metals are in serious trouble in
Pennsylvania, until recently, there have been no significant tax advantages, while any new industry which decided to locate in the state was given such preferences.
For a large new industry, e.g., the proposed Saturn automobile plant, those tax advantages are potentially enormous. They are matched by those being offered by Ohio,
Michigan, and other states.

The problem with using tax preferences to attact industry is that much of the empirical evidence available
indicates that these are not necessarily what industries
look for in a new location (Gray & Spina, 1980; Hansen,
1984; Peters, 1984). In fact, one of the things firms
say they most want in a location--the necessary public
works infrastructure to conduct business--is threatened
by the willingness of state and local governments to undermine their tax base. Thus, we have newspaper accounts
of firms leaving California after the passage of Proposition 13 because the reduced revenues available did not
provide sufficient funds to maintain quality public education, good roads, and all the other basic services
which local governments provide to business. In addition, not only do these tax incentives not necessarily
provide the most powerful incentives for industries but,
to the extent that they are widely employed, they reduce
the collective ability of the country to sustain and promote economic growth because of the absence of the necessary public capital. We run the risk of becoming a "nation in ruins" (Choate & Walter, 1981) faster than we
run the risk of becoming a "nation of hamburger stands."
Thus, as in so many policymaking situations, we have another instance in which the pursuit of individual rationality (here on the part of all subnational governments)
produces collective irrationality and a situation that
approaches the classic "tragedy of the commons" (Hardin,
1966).

An industrial or regional policy need not, of course,
be conducted in a competitive manner. There have been
experiences with noncompetitive programs in the United
States, most notably the Tennessee Valley Authority,
with the Appalachian Regional Commission being a somewhat less successful example. Similarly, the counter-
cyclical aid program for cities was a formula program
providing aid to cities heavily impacted by unemployment
rather than becoming a general subsidy for urban areas.
A fundamental question which must be asked about programs of this sort is whether they are intended to be social programs merely providing benefits for those living

in the areas or if they are intended to be economic development programs which will enable a depressed area to return to (or achieve for the first time) a high level of economic activity. While some of each form of aid may be desirable, too much emphasis on social benefits may reduce pressures for structural adjustment. This then comes back to the need for labor market programs which will ease the transition of workers from one type of employment to another. The American experience with manpower training programs has not been especially positive, but some positive incentives may be as necessary as the sanctions being imposed by the marketplace if change is to occur (Baumer & Van Horn, 1985). There are political problems in implementing regional policies of this sort with federal funds, given the already mentioned tendency not to reward particular regions or constituencies differentially. Just as sectoral industrial policies directed toward specific regions are difficult to implement politically, so too are regional policies unless there are overwhelming needs to do so, as was the case of the TVA and the Appalachian region.

In summary, there are a number of strategic choices that must be considered in thinking about industrial policy. These have been discussed primarily from their economic perspectives, but there are definite political choices involved as well. The type of policy that is the most feasible politically may not be the policy that will most effectively address the structural problems which are perceived to exist in the American economy, and which were the cause of the initial desire for an industrial policy. The decline of certain major industries because (at least in part) of their vulnerability to international competition triggered an interest in industrial policy. To address the problems of those industries, if indeed that is the policy option chosen, would require a targeted policy rather than a macrolevel strategy of "all bottoms rising on a rising tide." The fundamental political question, therefore, is whether such a highly directed and coherent policy would be possible within the political framework of the United States.

POLICYMAKING IN THE UNITED STATES

We have been arguing implicitly and to a lesser extent explicitly that the policymaking process of the United States is not conducive to the formulation and implementation of a comprehensive and integrated industrial policy, especially one which treats different industries in different parts of the country differently. There are five fundamental reasons for believing that such a program could not be adopted and successfully implemented in the United States: ideology, the parochial imperative, institutions, incrementalism, and economic structure.

Ideology

The simplest means of understanding why it may be difficult to have a successful industrial policy in the United
States is ideology. As Anthony King (1976) argued, when
discussing the apparent absence of economic intervention
by the federal government, the reason the United States
is different is that it wanted to be different. For the
advocates of a strong industrial policy, the bad news
may be that democracy works, and a general popular un-
ease about policies that intervene for the most part
through general and indirect means. Because of the number of indirect mechanisms for intervention, King saw
less government involvement than is actually present,
but did observe that fundamental point that there is an
ideology which might make a comprehensive industrial
strategy unpalatable to the majority of Americans.
    Elsewhere in this volume (Lauber), the need for an
ideological consensus in favor of government economic
planning for the success of government planning has been
well documented. Such a consensus certainly does not
exist in the United States. With the current strength
of conservative politics, there would appear to be less
consensus in favor of such interventions than might have
been present even ten years ago. Interestingly, therefore, at a time when some leaders of labor and even a
few in business have called for a retreat from traditional values about economic intervention, government--per-
haps accurately taking its cues from the voters--is even
more firmly entrenched in an anti-interventionist position. That anti-interventionist position extends even to
the point of removing supports from agriculture and from
small businesses which had been favored in government
policy for a number of years. Therefore, without that
consensus among business, labor, and government, any industrial policy which might be adopted would be prey to
many of the other weaknesses of policymaking that will
be documented below and, as we mentioned at the outset
of the discussion, any policy which might be adopted under those circumstances would be worse than nothing.

The Parochial Imperative

Industrial policy is inherently redistributive. It may
involve taking resources from the economy in general and
using them to support only certain industries. It may
involve taking money from consumers and giving it to certain industries and certain types of workers; estimates
are that the import restrictions on Japanese cars cost
American consumers several billion dollars. Industrial
policies may also involve moving resources from one geographical place to another; state and local industrial
policies are clearly intended to have that effect. Unfortunately, American politics is not very good at making

redistributive decisions, especially ones that involve advantaging one region over another. American politics is much better at making distributive decisions in which all participants and all parts of the country receive some share of the pie. This "parochial imperative" (Fitzgerald & Lipson, 1984) is very important for understanding the difficulties which would be encountered by advocates of industrial policy.

This parochial imperative is particularly evident in decision making in Congress. One school of thought about congressional behavior argues that one of the principal aims of any politician in office is to remain in office or advance to a higher office (Schlesinger, 1966), then the incentives of Congress can be seen as something other than making strong and controversial stances on policy issues. Rather, their most effective strategy may be to bring home the bacon from the pork barrel and to be as noncontroversial as possible (Fiorina, 1977; Mayhew, 1974). In other words, the incentives of members of Congress are to use the available public programs as a means of distributing largesse in order to demonstrate to the voters back home that they are effective legislators—at least effective in generating direct benefits for their constituents. Therefore, any public program is a target for conversion into a distributive program which would provide benefits to as many congressional districts as possible. Further, the ability to "log roll" across a range of programs makes it possible to convert more programs into distributive rather than redistributive programs. In short, the political process and the incentives available to politicians in those institutions tend to push toward general subsidy programs rather than more targeted programs (Shull, 1983).

Any industrial policy that is likely to be effective in producing significant change will have at least a moderate redistributive element. It will require taking from some segment of the population—defined in industrial or geographical terms—and giving it to others. This is as true if the policy is to pick winners as it would be if it were to bail out losers, although the redistributional elements would be more obvious in a bailout strategy. The fragmentation of the policymaking process makes it difficult to generate such redistributive decisions. The tendency is not to confront redistributive decisions directly but to make distributive decisions giving all concerned parties a portion of the available benefits. This is an excellent political strategy for it creates coalitions in favor of the policies but, in so doing, makes doing anything through government quite expensive and to some degree counterproductive. For example, the Model Cities Program, which was conceptualized to aid a few extremely deprived major cities, was extended to cover over 150 cities, including such metropolises as Alma, Georgia. Similarly, the

Elementary and Secondary Education Act of 1965 was intended to benefit school districts most in need because
of poor tax bases and high proportions of disadvantaged
students, but it was quickly converted into a general
subsidy for elementary and secondary education for virtually all school districts and even for private schools.
Therefore, any attempt to develop an industrial policy
that would be other than a general subsidy for industry--
many of which already exist through the tax system--would
be difficult to sustain politically. If a program with
the "pork barrel" characteristics described above were
put into place, it would in all likelihood be very expensive and probably not produce the type of structural
economic change desired. This is especially true if the
intent of the program were to try to pick the industries
of the future rather than to maintain the industries of
the past.

Institutions

In attempting to understand the apparent failure of the
United States to develop a workable policy about regional population growth and associated matters of regional
policy, as contrasted with the relative success of several European countries, James Sundquist (1978) developed
four criteria which he thought were crucial for explaining the differences:

1. Differential Levels of Bureaucratic Capabilitiy;
2. Differential Degrees of Bureaucratic Discipline;
3. Differences in the Institutional Environment of
   Planning; and
4. Differences in the Stability and Authority of
   Party Programs.

The same problems in the policymaking process apply to
making industrial policy, especially an industrial policy which is an attempt to implement a strategy for
planned change.

Bureaucratic Capability. First, it can be argued that
the United States does not have as capable a group of
senior administrators in charge of making and implementing policy as do the European countries. This is not an
attack on the capabilities of the American career civil
service but, rather, a reflection on the use of political appointees in many senior administrative posts. This
means that the majority of administrators in the most
responsible posts are amateurs. The "government of
strangers" (Heclo, 1978a) which exists in the United
States means that the large majority of senior policy
posts are occupied by people whose tenure in office av-
erages less than two years. Many of these "amateurs"
are quite capable but simply may not be knowledgeable
about the procedures and folkways of government. They

also may be quite impatient and unwilling to invest the
time needed to develop a detailed program; their time-
table in office is simply different from that of a career public servant. There is a tendency to assume that
people brought into government from the private sector,
especially from business, will be wiser and more capable
than career officials, but a good deal of evidence indicates that they frequently fail to understand the com-
plexity of their tasks (Peters, 1985). Further, if a
comprehensive and coordinated policy is sought, it may
be well to have it made by people who have developed a
working relationship among themselves and with the rest
of the machinery of government, and who have their only
career ambitions within the civil service.

Bureaucratic Disciplines. Not only are American senior
bureaucrats frequently less talented and experienced
than their European counterparts, but they may also be
less disciplined. This absence of discipline arises in
two ways. The first, as mentioned by Sundquist (1978),
is that the temporary public servants who come and go
with a president actually may not be commited to the program of the president but may be in Washington to have
their own "intellectual fling" and promote their own
ideological interests (p. 75). The Reagan administration has imposed greater ideological control on its appointees than have most other administrations but, even
in this administration, there have been those who have
tried to go their own way. This lack of discipline can
only increase as the public bureaucracy is made increasingly political and even the career service is opened to
greater political involvement, e.g., the opening of all
general Senior Executive Service positions to political
appointees. The assumption of some analysts that the
ability of a president to appoint several thousand people
to office--as contrasted with the few hundred that most
political executives can apoint--will ensure greater uni-
formity and control is in practice quite fallacious. Ap-
pointments are not made only on the agreement of an individual with the program of the president, if indeed
that level of agreement is known, but on a variety of political and other criteria. Once appointed, the individuals in question may well go off and "marry the na-
tives." As one Kennedy staffer put it, "Everybody believes in democracy until they get to the White House"
(Cronin, 1970).
The second manifestation of the lack of discipline
is the tendency of those working in the federal government not to think of what they are doing as related to
the whole range of federal policies but as an activity
in itself. American public policymaking and the American bureaucracy is highly fragmented. The traditional
conceptualization of the policy process as a series of
differentiated "iron triangles" may no longer be completely

descriptive of a more complex policymaking system (Heclo, 1978b; Jordan, 1981). However, the career structures and the major political incentives exist within single organizations, or organizational networks, rather than within the civil service or the public sector as a whole. Given that some of the existing issue networks relevant to industrial policy are organized around single commodities rather than around business and industry as a whole (see the comments below on the nature of the organization involved in policymaking), the possiblities of developing a cooperative and integrated industrial policy are diminished.

The Institutional Environment of Planning. Related to the lack of discipline extending across various governments in the United States is the complex institutional environment within which policy is made. As any number of analysts have noted, the best way to understand American government is not as a government but as a set of governments; it is government by nonconsensual directions (Peters, 1981). The fragmentation of policymaking into a number of functionally-defined subgovernments--containing congressional subcommittees, interest groups, and bureaus--means that it is difficult to find a set of integrated priorities reflected in the policies of the the federal government. To some extent, the only person capable of developing such a well-ordered set of priorities is the president but he, too, may find his policymaking efforts very fragmented (Rose, 1975). In addition, not only is government fragmented by policy area but it is further fragmented into the three branches of government. This separation means that, even if agreement could be reached within the executive branch over what sort of an industrial policy to follow, such a consensus could be overturned by Congress or by the courts. Finally, a great deal of federal policy is implemented by the state and local governments so that, even if the federal government were to develop a consensus about what should be done in industrial policy, a number of subsidiary decisions would have to be made in the appropriate manner for that policy to go into effect as intended. Such agreement up and down the ladder of government is unlikely (Pressman & Wildavsky, 1984). In short, planning and policy formulation in the federal government have an air of great indeterminacy and the associated fragmentation may mean that little effective and coordinated policy can be developed.

Even if the federal government can make up its collective mind, it will still depend upon state and local governments for implementation, especially for most social and economic policies such as those envisaged by industrial policies. Further, the federal government itself may make up its mind in a number of different ways depending upon which particular agencies and sub-

governments are doing the deciding; at least eight federal departments and numerous agencies are involved in
promoting foreign trade for example (Steinbach & Pierce,
1984).   Sundquist (1978) makes a clear contrast between
this disorderly picture and the ability of European governments to make decisions with relative ease and to implement them through their own agents. Of course, it is
a great oversimplification to treat all European governments as identical and to assume such ease in all policymaking environments. However, even in European countries
with greater divisions of policymaking and implementation
than most, such as West Germany, there is still greater
ease in reaching a decision and greater certainty that
the decision will remain the decision as it is being implemented.

Stability and Authority of Party Programs. Finally, the
American political system is not particularly good at
translating pledges made by political parties into action. The major exception to that generalization is, of
course, Ronald Reagan, who has alarmed many people who
voted for him by doing exactly what he said he would do.
The discussion of "responsible" political parties goes
back as far as Woodrow Wilson (1888) and has been a frequent topic of discussion since that time (Ranney & Kendall, 1956). The European political parties which the
American reformers would like to emulate have machinery
for collective policy choice which American parties do
not have. This means that, once in office, any and all
members are likely to be obliged to follow the party's
program and the mechanisms of cabinet government can be
used to enforce that discipline on those in government.
This does not mean that the promises made in a campaign
will necessarily be implemented; there are any number of
other barriers to that happening (Rose, 1974, 1984). It
does mean, however, that there will be less internal opposition within the governing party.
     In the United States, by way of contrast, the deci-
sions taken by a president or his political party are
not binding on his own appointees. Those appointees
will have their own political constituencies and may not
be answerable to the president or even to the party for
their political futures. The decentralization of the
nomination process and all the machinery of political
parties makes it difficult if not impossible to enforce
any meaningful party discipline. Thus, policymakers in
the federal government, and certainly those in the state
governments, may behave in manners quite contrary to the
intentions of a president of the same political party and
the stated objectives of the party program, and they can
do so with little fear for their political future. The
nonideological character of American political parties
has been cited as one of their virtues but, in the context of policymaking, it is also a substantial weakness.

This institutional analysis of policymaking in the United States has pointed to certain deficiencies in the process of making policy. When these are summed, they indicate that it is unlikely that a coordinated policy for intervention in the industrial sectors of the economy could be developed. The multiplicity of actors and the lack of coordinating mechanisms among them would militate in favor of fragmented and possibly contradictory approaches to the problem of economic planning. As Walters (1984) put it, "the institutional basis for guiding a coherent industrial policy for the United States has yet to be created" (p. 39).

Incrementalism

It should also be noted that an industrial policy has some of the characteristics of a large-scale policy as described by Schulman (1980). That is, any small-scale, incremental interventions may produce little or no good and may produce the phenomenon which we have described elsewhere as "bleeding" (Hogwood & Peters, 1985). Unfortunately, however, the American political system is much better at producing incremental changes than the larger scale policy innovations which may be required for effectiveness. There have been some notable successes in innovations (Polsby, 1984; Schwartz, 1983), but incrementalism remains the preferred mode of policymaking.

The predilection of the American political system to produce incremental solutions is to some degree related to the ideological and institutional points raised above. In the first place, the relatively conservative political ideology mentioned above does not favor large-scale public actions, especially in the area of economic policy. A slower evolutionary approach is much more acceptable. Likewise, the fragmentation of political decision making and the number of actors who have to be brought into any coalition for change will mean that it is easier to produce small change than to produce large-scale change. However, this may be exactly the wrong approach to take when attempting to address a structural problem such as the (presumed) need for an industrial policy.

The Economic Structure

Some aspects of industrial organization and the political manifestation of that economic structure are also important for understanding the development, or lack of it, of an industrial policy in the United States. Hall (1983), when discussing the comparative policymaking capacity of political systems in Europe noted that the nature of the social and economic system for which the policy was being made was important in predicting the

success of the policies themselves. In particular, a
more disciplined and unified set of pressure groups
within the area of economic policy will make it more
feasible to develop a program which, if not entirely
pleasing to all interests concerned, will certainly make
reaching some agreement about such a policy more acceptable. McKay and Grant (1983) make a similar point in
discussing the comparative success of industrial policies in OECD nations. They argue that the existence of
good channels of communications between government and
economic actors, and among those economic actors themselves, is important for developing successful industrial policies. They do not argue directly that the integration of sets of economic actors is necessary, but
that is certainly implied by the case studies from which
they build their generalizations (Estrin & Holmes, 1983;
Hills, 1983; Sidenius, 1983). In a similar vein, Olson
(1982) has argued that fragmented, small interest groups
in a politico-economic system will produce inefficiencies in policymaking which will threaten the economic
performance of such societies. Further, as we argue
above, such a system of interest groups is presumed to
favor older entrenched interests; this in itself may be
seen as slowing the rate of economic growth.

Unfortunately for those who see an industrial policy as essential for the economic future of the United
States, the type of unified and coordinated interest
group population which may be beneficial for economic
policymaking does not exist in this country. On the
side of industry, there is a tendency for each industry
to pursue its own strategy rather than developing peak
organizations which can bargain effectively for all industry or business interests. There are some groups
which attempt to do so such as the National Association
of Manufacturers and the Chamber of Commerce, but there
are so many other sectoral and industrial groups that
these umbrella organizations are less effective than
might be expected, given the presumed power of business
interests in American politics. Further, the structure
of policymaking in the federal government, with the
large number of specialized networks organized around
the decentralized structures in Congress and the federal
bureaucracy, means that it is difficult to develop an
integrated set of demands from industry. Instead, trade
associations tend to be more dominant than the umbrella
organizations.

Much the same degree of fragmentation is apparent
in organized labor. There is the national federation of
the AFL-CIO, but it does not contain a number of the
largest and most powerful unions most affected by international competition such as the United Auto Workers and
the Teamsters Union. There is no history of national
bargaining about wages and prices as is true in most
European countries, so that there is no tradition of labor

speaking for anything other than the relatively limited interests within its own industry. Likewise, there is no single body which can deliver labor in an agreement over industrial policy, labor market policy, wage and price policy, or whatever. Labor is also decentralized within the unions with locals having more power to make autonomous decisions than would be true within most European unions, with the possible exception of those in Great Britain. Again, this can be contrasted to many European countries where the Spitzenverbände in labor can speak for the memberships and bargain effectively for labor as an entity.

The above discussion of the importance of bargaining structures of labor and management for industrial policy points rather obviously to the importance of corporatist political structures for making policies of this type. We do not want to get into an arcane discussion of the exact meaning of the term "corporatism" or the multiple varieties of that form of policymaking (Heisler, 1979; Katzenstein, 1984, Schmitter, 1974). However, we are interested in the degree to which there are a few peak organizations with close ties to government which can speak for their respective interests and which are capable of developing a relatively coherent industrial policy. This is in obvious contrast to the decentralized and somewhat chaotic political arena of the United States (Salisbury, 1979). Interestingly, some structures of this type appear to be developing in the American states, as the states recognize the importance of agreements of industrial policy for their own futures (Hudson, Hyde, & Carroll, n.d.). Nothing of that sort has yet developed at the federal level, and arguably little effective can be done in industrial policy until there is some fundamental economic agreement of that sort.

A corporatist arrangement, or something approaching it no matter what it is called, would do several things for policymaking in the United States. The first would be to directly link interest groups and the public sector in something other than the traditional manner. The tradition of pluralism and "interest group liberalism" in the United States makes such a direct linkage and the role of the interest group in promoting any form of collective interest problematic. The politics of interest groups in the United States has been the politics of access (Peters, 1984b). There are close and direct linkages between interest groups and individual agencies, but these relationships tend to be singular and exclusive. This can be contrasted with the more professional and public role of interest groups in societies having some form of corporate pluralism (Kvavik, 1978). The singular and exclusive role of interest groups, as noted above, will only tend to perpetuate much of the existing structure of industry rather than produce significant

and needed change (Cohen, 1985; Olson, 1982). One should
not expect a full-blown corporatist arrangement to develop quickly in the United States, but the need for
greater cooperation and coordination in economic policy
is increasingly evident.

Another institutional innovation that has been proposed for dealing with problems of industrial policy and
for escaping some of the bonds of the interest group
structure is to develop an independent industrial policy
board or bank. This has been seen as functioning with
some of the autonomy which now characterizes the Federal
Reserve Board. Such independent and quasi-autonomous
organizations are an increasing feature of public policymaking in the United States and most other industrialized countries (Mosher, 1980; Sharkansky, 1978). As
attractive as such independence might appear, the effect
would be to remove two important areas of economic policy from political control and accountability, while some
argue that one is more than enough. And would Congress
be willing to allow a comprehensive national planning
and management agency to function so autonomously (Etzioni, 1983)? As is so often the case, the "quick fix" of
institutional change may be insufficient to meet the
real needs of the policymaking system.

CONCLUSIONS

If one is thinking about the development of an industrial policy for the United States, there appear to be a
number of obstacles to success. The first and perhaps
most important is the real desirability of such a policy
on economic grounds. There is some writing arguing for
the necessity for such a policy, while critics of the
economic right and left have raised a number of doubts
about the efficacy of such an approach. Some of the
critics have gone so far as to argue that there really
is no problem, and the American economy is actually
functioning quite well.

There are political problems for industrial policy
as well. In the first place, the political structures
and traditions of the United States would make it difficult to implement a comprehensive and redistributive
policy. The political realities of policy formulation
may be such that a policy that could be adopted through
the normal channels of policymaking in the United States
might not be better than no policy at all, assuming that
the purpose is to develop a well-integrated attack on
real and/or perceived economic problems. In the first
place, there is no single organization within the federal government that is really responsible for such an approach to economic policy; as with policymaking at the
state level, the problem may be too many policies rather
than not enough. Second, state and local governments
have begun to play the economic development game in a

very big way and would probably be unwilling to stop
playing that game, even if they can be shown that their
collective efforts may not be productive. Congress may
labor under an equally "parochial imperative." The tendency to convert as many programs as possible into distributive, "pork barrel" problems may lessen the effectiveness of an industrial policy. Finally, the structure of interest groups and their relationships with a
fragmented policymaking system will tend to lessen the
likelihood of an effective industrial policy being enacted. The net result is that any industrial policy
that might be enacted would tend to be expensive, cum-
bersome, and probably quite ineffective. In other
words, if I wanted to get there, I wouldn't start from
here.

5
Interest Groups, Parties, and Economic Growth in the American States

Jeffrey E. Cohen
and Gregory G. Brunk

INTRODUCTION

For the better part of a decade, the American industrial
complex has been suffering. By suffering we mean that
it has been in a state of economic decline. Imports
have increased their share of domestic markets, while
exports have decreased, creating a massive trade deficit.
The number of jobs in key industries, such as steel and
automobiles, has contracted and productivity levels have
stagnated. These represent only some of the more visible
signs of decline.
Many causes for this decline have been cited. Unfair foreign competition, high labor costs, declining
productivity, comparative lack of investment and savings,
and the slowness of giant corporations to commit to product innovation have all been offered as reasons for the
sorry state of the economy.
This economic decline has caused great concern among
both the leaders of the nation and the mass public. In
the 1970s, a new term came to the fore signaling increased
concern with economic performance, "reindustrialization."
Political scientist Kenneth Dolbeare (1982) offers a
useful definition:

> Reindustrialization means the development of a
> whole new and technologically advanced capital base
> (plants, machinery, transportation systems, etc.)
> for the production of goods and services in the
> United States. It is an all-encompassing approach
> to managing the economy that would direct fiscal,
> monetary, and other policies toward this single,
> overarching goal. (p. 102)

In this essay a theory that may have important implications for our understanding of the sources of economic
growth will be considered. The theory is Mancur Olson's
political economy of growth as presented in his major
work, The Rise and Decline of Nations (1982). Very
simply, Olson argues that the incentives to create

69

interest groups leads to certain politico-economic arrangements which hamper economic performance. The political economy acts to shift resources from some sectors of the economy into the sectors that these politico-economic arrangements protect.

OLSON'S MODEL

Olson's model is quite elegant and provocative, in part because it is based on a microlevel, rational theory of political organization first advanced in his book, The Logic of Collective Action (1965). In order to understand his theory of economic growth, we must begin with an understanding of his logic of collective action.

Olson begins with the standard economic rationality assumption frequently employed in the public choice literature. People are assumed to be rational and will emerge in an activity only if the benefits outweigh the costs. Given the opportunity to get a free ride, a person will not contribute or pay other kinds of costs. Getting a free ride means being able to receive the benefits of an action, in this case a government policy, without participating to secure the benefit. The implication of economic rationality and getting a free ride is that people seeking political benefits will be hampered when they try to form interest groups to support their cause because most political benefits are not exclusive. Therefore, to attract members, interest groups often have to resort to side payments only members can receive. Famous side payments include discounts on goods, vacations, publications, and group insurance programs.

Small groups are more easily formed than large ones. Individuals receive a greater benefit in small groups because there are fewer people with whom to share the benefits. These large individual shares may be big enough to offset the cost of participating in the small group, thereby serving as an incentive to join the group.[1]

In his later work, The Rise and Decline of Nations, Olson (1982) pushes the analysis begun in The Logic of Collective Action to its implications for the economy and the polity. First of all, one finds more small groups than large groups in a stable society. When one applies the logic of contribution mentioned above to a group's contribution to society's wealth, it may be possible again to get a free ride. That is, it may make more sense for a group to try to increase its share of society's wealth, thereby benefiting its members, than to help increase society's wealth, which would benefit nonmembers as well as members. Thus, one finds a redistribution of wealth from society and the unorganized, such as taxpayers, consumers, or the poor, toward the small, organized interests. Such a society resembles

Schattschneider's (1960) description of group politics
in the United States. Certain inefficiencies result
which limit economic growth and expansion.

Olson also tells us that old, politically entrenched
interests may be protected and survive threatening economic circumstances through this politico-economic system. Another inefficiency is built into the economic
system as resources are directed into old or marginal
economic sectors at the expense of newer and expanding
sectors.

In order for such a system to survive, political
stability is required. When the political system is
overturned, for example, through wars, these politico-
economic ties may be broken, and more efficient markets
may function for a time, until new politico-economic
ties of the sort mentioned above are established. Apart
from such massive dislocations to the political system
through war, only a system with large, encompassing organizations may overcome or moderate the tendency to politico-economic ties and its resulting economic stagnation.

Finally, only when encompassing interests exist will
society function in an economically efficient manner.
Encompassing interests have an incentive to increase society's wealth because they cannot increase the wealth
of their members by increasing their share of the existing pie--by definition, encompassing interests include
very large segments of society.

EMPIRICAL IMPLICATIONS OF THE MODEL

One of the great strengths of Olson's model is that empirical predictions may be generated and, to Olson's
credit, he attempts to test his ideas with many different
kinds of data, from the discursive and anecdotal to the
quantitative. Olson's model suggests that the stronger
the interest group system, the more slowly the economy
will grow. Further, war and the stability of a political
system tap basic characteristics about the strength of
the interest group system.

Olson defines stability as the age of a polity and
argues that the older and more stable a political system,
the longer the interest group system has had to develop.
Much of Olson's analysis compares the fifty American
states. He argues that one measure of stability, or age,
is the length of time since a state entered the union.
Hence, Olson credits the great economic growth of the
"Sunbelt" versus the "Snowbelt" to this age factor.

Olson also suggests that wars may undermine and de-
stroy the system of protected interests, at least for
the losers. Therefore, one should witness rapid economic
growth after the loss of a major war. There is some
evidence to support this point. Olson mentions the
German and Japanese economic miracles in the post-World

War II period, and credits slow British growth to the
(un)fortunate case of Britain being on the winning side.
Organski and Kugler (1977) document quantitatively for
a larger class of cases that losing nations seem to re-
cover economically in short order after the cessation of
war.

In a blend of the aging and war factors, Olson also
argues that the more recent economic growth of the South
is a function of its occupation by the North during reconstruction, an occupation which destroyed the old politico-economic system, and in a sense allowed the South
to start over economically. However, this point bears
further discussion. The economic growth of the South
did not proceed until about 100 years after the end of
the Civil War. Surely, Olson does not intend such a
long lag in his theory (Ray, 1984). Why, for instance,
did it take so long for southern economic expansion?
Part of the reason may lie in the fact that, though the
North did win and some patterns of the Old South were
wiped out, the racial system of the South was not al-
tered fundamentally. Blacks did not rise econmically
above their slave days and, though free, were not ac-
corded equal treatment, as the history of the civil
rights movement surely attests.

Nevertheless, Olson has given us much to mull over.
The rest of this essay will be dedicated to Olson's
quantitative tests of his theory, tests which seem very
robust but, as we will argue, can be improved upon.

QUANTITATIVE TESTS OF OLSON'S MODEL

Olson's theory is amenable to testing, and he performed
one of the first tests of his own theory (Olson, 1982,
1983). Others have also attempted to test the theory
using time series (Pryor, 1983), cross-national (Choi,
1983; Murrell, 1983; Pryor, 1983), and comparative American state (Dye, 1980) designs. In this discussion, we
focus on the comparative American state studies. Much
of the discussion of those studies is relevant to the
other designs as well.

One can state Olson's guiding hypothesis this way:
There is an inverse relationship between economic growth
and the strength of interest groups. Or, more formally,
one can state the relationship with a regression style
equation:
$$Y = a-bX+e$$
where
  Y = economic growth
  a = intercept
  b = regression coefficient
  X = interest group strength
  e = error term (unmeasured variables that may also
      affect economic growth)

In his tests using the American state data, Olson
uses three measures of economic growth: growth of manufacturing income, 1965-78; growth of income of labor and
proprietors, 1965-80; and growth of nonfarm income, 1965
-78. All are exponentially transformed in the equations
for use in the regressions, and the latter two are also
expressed in per capita form. Olson's equations show
essentially the same results no matter the form of the
economic growth variable. Dye (1980) reports findings
similar to Olson's without using the transformed growth
measures. Both Dye and Olson demonstrate that all of
the growth measures are similar by showing that they
are highly intercorrelated.   ·

The measurement of the equation's right-hand side
variables, interest group strength, is controversial.
For interest group strength, Olson relies upon three
variables: age of the state, urbanization, and unionization. Continuous existence of the state is a measure
of political stability, and Olson argues that the older
the state the longer the time that interests have had
to form and, thus, affect the government and the economy.
To correct for the southern Civil War experience and the
argued effects of defeat in war and occupation by other
powers, Olson also employs a dummy variable for the
southern states. Urbanization is employed as a measure
of diversity, with the guiding assumption that greater
diversity leads to more and various interest groups.
Also, though not mentioned by Olson, urbanization is related to political activity that may exhibit itself as
interest group activity. Further, unionization rates
measure only one of the strongest of the interest groups.
Each of the variables, in various forms, tends to work
similarly in Olson's tests, however, and Olson shows
that they are correlated.

However, one must begin to question some of these
measures on grounds of logic as well as distance from
the core concept of interest group strength. First,
consider the unionization variable. Olson finds that
states with higher unionization rates have slower growth
than states with lower unionization rates. Initially,
this appears consistent with his model, but consider another implication of his model.

His model is dynamic, that is, it is about processes
that develop over time. The unionization variable that
he uses, for example, the percent of the nonfarm labor
force that was unionized in 1964, is not a time-related
variable but is a static, cross-sectional one. To spe-
cify his model more correctly, one would use the rate of
change in unionization, just as the dependent variable,
economic growth, is expressed in rates of change.

Focusing on changes in the interest group variables
leads one to note that unionization rates have declined
nationally for a number of decades. That is, unions as
an interest have become weaker. Olson's model would then

predict increased economic growth, at least nationally. Our concern should be with the rates of decline or gain among unions across the states over the time period. This will allow a dynamic specification of Olson's model rather than the static, cross-sectional specification that he uses. For example, from 1970 to 1978, union membership fell from 28.0 to 23.6 percent nationally. However, this drop was not uniform throughout the nation. Nevada, Utah, Washington, and California registered declines of 7.0 percent or greater; while other states, such as Alaska, Delaware, and Missippi, saw rates drop less than 1.0 percent. Still others, Hawaii, New York, Rhode Island, and Vermont, witnessed increases in union membership.[2] This variable affects economic growth as we have suggested: states where union declines were greatest exhibited the greatest gains in economic growth.

Table 5.1 demonstrates this point. States were divided into two groups, those with weak and strong unions in 1970. This division is used because it is likely that union membership losses will have more impact on states with strong unions than those with weaker unions. In other words, weak unions should be less of a drag on the economy than strong unions. I use 21 percent as the division between strong and weak unions because this neatly divides the nation into two equally sized groups.

TABLE 5.1
THE RELATIONSHIP BETWEEN CHANGE IN UNION STRENGTH AND ECONOMIC GROWTH, 1970-1980

Union Membership in 1970*
% Change

Growth	Below 21%				Above 21%			
	All	-4.0+	-3.9 to 0.0	0.1+	All	-4.0+	-3.0 to 0.0	0.1+
Mean %	4.95	5.34	4.73	--	3.07	3.56	2.56	1.93
n	25	5	20	--	24	14	7	3

*Alaska is excluded. The growth variable is percent increase in personal income, 1970-78 from Dye, 1980, pp. 1090-91.

One can see on the table that, for both groups, states where union membership fell off the most exhibited the greatest gains in economic growth and, as suggested, the relationship is more pronounced for the states with strong unions in 1970 than states with weaker unions. The dynamic critique should hold for the urbanization variable as well.

Unions are only one of many interests in society, and the strength of unions may not be a sensitive measure of the overall strength of interests in society. Consider, for example, the influence of the business community as an interest vis a vis the power of unions. They should be inversely related much of the time. One may see this, for example, during the Reagan years which saw a shift in government policies away from unions and toward business, even on such pro-union governmental bodies as the National Labor Relations Board. The point is that unionization rates are not a good measure of the general vitality of organized interests. Either one must develop such a measure or build a multivariate model that includes measures of the strength of all the important organized interest sectors of the political economy. Therefore, not only is the unionization variable static when it should be dynamic, but Olson's tests are more often than not univariate when they should be multivariate.

Olson also measures urbanization statically and finds the awkward result that urbanization in 1980 is a better predictor of economic growth in the 1965-78 period than urbanization in 1970 (Olson, 1982, p. 106). One must ask, what does urbanization measure? Obviously, it measures many things: the nature of the economy (urbanized states are not likely to be as heavily agricultural as less urbanized states), the diversity of the population, wealth, and many other factors. Urbanization as a variable is ambiguous in that it may tap many things. How sensitive is urbanization to the interest group environment, which is Olson's main concern?

Age is also a controversial measure of interest group strength. However, it proves to be the most powerful of Olson's variables, and Dye (1980) also finds age a strong predictor. Olson views age, or the number of continuous years since the state entered or reentered the union, as a measure of how long interests have had a chance to form. He argues that the older the state, the more aggregately powerful interests will be.

The age variable presents some problems, though. Olson assumes, through this measurement, that interest group strength falls across the states uniformly. That is, at age 10, any two states will possess interests of equal strength. This is a dubious assumption. It may be more likely that the effects of aging vary with the type of economy. For instance, one may hypothesize that aging in less diverse and smaller states produces Olson's economic effects more rapidly than in more diverse and larger states. Last, and perhaps most important, what does age measure? This is a most difficult question. Like time, age is ubiquitous and measures anything and everything that ages. Thomas Dye (1980, pp. 1102-05) has tried to address this problem.[3]

Using causal modeling, Dye finds that age corre-
lates with unionization (the older the more unionized)
and with highway expenditures (the older the less spent on
highways)(p. 1104). Dye interprets this as partial support for Olson. Olson uses both unionization and age as
measures of interest strength, and they are indeed related. However, Dye considers highway expenditures to be
a measure of state government investment in the infrastructure as a state policy. And the age/highway expenditure correlation is stronger than the age/urbanization
one. However, in support of Olson, strong highway lob-
bies may have a significant effect on highway spending.
Nice (1984) finds that states with strong interests
spend more on highways than states with weaker interests
(p. 193).

On the whole, it is not clear what age actually
measures. It probably taps to some degree the strength
of interests, but it may also tap other nonrelated processes that also happen to increase or decrease with age.
Better measures of interest group strength are needed in
order to provide a convincing test of Olson's theory.

AN ALTERNATIVE EXPLANATION

While the deductive logic behind Olson's model is allur-
ing, tests of the model have been less than definitive.
As has been demonstrated, existing empirical tests are
deficient on a number of grounds; static tests are used
when dynamic ones are called for and weak measurement of
key theoretical variables abounds. Also limiting the ex-
tant tests is the need to control for alternative explanations. Other theories may provide more powerful explanations of growth, and they might even displace Olson's variables as predictors.

Party Strength

One possible competitor to the interest group theory is
one based on party strength. In his famous study,
Schattschneider (1960) argues that there are two types
of politics, "pressure politics and party politics" (p.
20). Political scientists often view the two types as
inversely related. That is, one tends to find strong
parties where interest groups are comparatively weak.
Documentation of this is not definitive, due mostly to
the lack of good measures of interest group strength,
but numerous studies make this claim (Froman, 1966, p.
955; Nice, 1984, p. 188; Zeigler & vanDalen, 1971, p.
127). The causal relationship between party and interest group strength is not clear, but some tend to feel
strong parties help to immunize the political system
from interest groups, and force interest groups to use
parties as middlemen in their attempts to secure favorable policies from the government (Schattschneider, 1960).

Olson (1982) also refers to parties, but only in passing in his discussion of encompassing interests.

> Encompassing interests have some incentive to make the society in which they operate more prosperous, and an incentive to redistribute income to their members with as little excess burden as possible, and to cease such redistribution unless the amount redistributed is substantial in relation to the social costs of the redistribution. (p. 53)

This incentive derives from the fact that increasing the benefits of members of the encompassing interest by extracting more from society is not possible because of the size of the encompassing interest. Instead, to increase its members' benefits, the encompassing interest must try to increase the wealth of the whole society.

While Olson considers that parties may be encompassing interests, he dismisses this as a possibility in the United States. Instead, he focuses on the standard arguments about the parochial nature of the parties and their relative lack of vitality when compared to other nations (1982, pp. 50-52). However, his argument is based on the national parties. There is evidence that parties vary in their vitality across the states and, in some states, the party system may begin to approach the levels of strength necessary to act as an encompassing interest.[4] At least this is theoretically possible.

Parties may be thought of as encompassing interests. To measure party vitality, we rely on the standard measure of state party competition, the Ranney Index (Ranney, 1971). Though there are many dimensions to party strength, such as organizational strength (Gibson et al., 1983), party competition is most relevant for present purposes because it taps the strength of the party system as well as the comparative strengths of the individual parties.

In order to be consistent with our emphasis on dynamics, we created a measure of the changing level of party competition by first folding the Ranney Index of party competition for 1971 and 1980 and subtracting the 1971 value from the 1980 value.[5]

There is modest support for the proposition that states getting more competitive also display faster-growing economies; for example, of states increasing their competitiveness by .0069 or more, personal income growth rates averaged 4.5 percent (Dye, 1980, pp. 1090-91).[6] Similarly, states with little change in competition (measured by the range of .0069 to -.0069) also witnessed growth of 4.5 percent. However, states getting less competitive (that is, -.0070 or greater) saw growth of only 3.0 percent.

INTERESTS, PARTIES, AND GROWTH

In this section we focus on the comparative effects of
political parties and interest groups on economic growth.
Such a focus has implications beyond just a test of Olson's hypothesis, it is also a test of the impact of politically organizing people in different ways.

The literature on comparative state policy has focused quite heavily on the role of parties in determining policies and converting demands into policy. This
literature has, on the other hand, given relatively little attention to the role of interest groups. Olson's
ideas and this essay should attest to the need for more
research on the policy affects of interest groups (see
also Nice, 1984).

Relying on Olson's study and the comparative policy
literature will also lead one to the conclusion that it
makes a difference whether politics is organized around
interests or parties. For instance, Olson (1982) argues
that economic growth, if unencumbered by interests, has
a net positive effect on society and, further, that it
is optimal. Another way of saying this is that, while
not everyone will benefit from economic growth, no one
will suffer, that is, no one will be made poorer.

However, such situations are not always politically
palatable. Consider the debate of recent years of who
has been sharing in the boom years of 1983-84. Critics
argue that the gap between rich and poor has widened,
and moderate critics argue that if the poor are not getting poorer, the rich are getting richer, and the poor
are not sharing in the new wealth.

In such situations, organizations that can mobilize
and articulate the concerns of the "poor" or the "have
nots" become important, especially to the "have nots."
This is a role that the parties traditionally have played.
The parties, in these circumstances, may offer economic
growth and a fairer distribution of the new wealth, i.e.,
redistribution. And some data already presented indicate that party competition and economic growth are at
least mildly related. While the linkage between political organization, growth, and the distribution of wealth
will not be tested in this essay, findings about the
relative impact of the parties and interest groups have
major implications for the questions of redistribution.

Let us consider the impact of interest groups with
some of the refinements of Olson's equation that were offered above. Two refinements are important: that the
measures of interests have some dynamic qualities, and
that they tap the strength of interests more directly
than Olson's measure. We use two measures of interest
group strength not used by Olson. The first is Nice's
(1984) indicator of interest group success. Nice's
measure is a calculation of the percentage of times that
congressional candidates endorsed by six major interest

groups from 1972 through 1978 won their election contests. In all, Nice reports over 4,800 endorsements of which 68 percent of the endorsed candidates won (p. 186). The expectation behind this measure is that states with more successful interest groups should display slower growth rates.

The second measure is the change in the percentage of nonagricultural workers who belonged to labor unions from 1970 to 1980. Also, the union membership in 1970 is used as a control for the varying impact of membership change in weak and strong union states. We retain Olson's age variable, measured as the number of years since the state entered or reentered the union.

The effects of these interest group variables on economic growth, here defined as the percent change in personal income from 1970 to 1980, can be modeled with the following multiple regression equation:

$$Y = a + bX_1 + bX_2 + bX_3 + bX_4$$

where:

Y = percent change in personal income 1970-80
a = constant
b - regression coefficient
X_1= percent change in union membership, 1970-80
X_2= percent union membership, 1980
X_3= Nice's interest group success index
X_4= years since entry or reentry into the union.

The results for the equation are:

$$Y = 6.03 - 3.5(.76) - 1.78(.29) - .27(.05) - .24(10)$$

$$R^2 = .67 \text{ Adjusted } R^2 = .64$$

$$F = 21.6$$

All variables in the equation are significant and point in the correct direction (for the equation, b's are stated and their standard errors are in parentheses). That is, one finds more growth in younger states, those with the greatest declines in unions, those with weak unions, and states where interests are least successful. Like the Olson and Dye models, this interest group model is quite robust. The impact of measurement is significant if one compares the results here with Olson's. While they are similar, the results here are much stronger. Olson's highest R^2 (explained variance) was .59; most were in the .25 to .40 range, while this R^2 is .67, surely a considerable improvement.

The next equation adds changing party competition. Here one should expect that states with party systems that are getting more competitive will display greater growth levels.

$$Y = a + bX_1 + bX_2 + bX_3 + bX_4 + bX_5$$

where

Y = percent change in personal income 1970-80
a = constant
b = regression coefficient

X_1 = percent change in union membership, 1970-80
X_2 = percent union membership, 1970
X_3 = Nice's interest group success index
X_4 = years since entry or reentry into the union
X_5 = change in the Ranney party competittion index,
　　　　1980-1971

The results of the equation are:

$$Y = 6.01-3.5(.76)-1.70(.31)-.28(.05)-.25(10)$$
$$-15.7(25.5)$$

$$R^2 = .67 \quad \text{Adjusted } R^2 = .63$$
$$F = 17.1$$

This equation performed similarly to the earlier one, and the addition of the party variable had no impact. At least in this test, and using this measure of the party system, parties seem to have no impact on economic growth once one has taken into account the impact of the interest group system.

　　These results have some important theoretical implications. They seem to confirm the general feeling that current parties are not as powerful as interest groups in many areas of policy. The past two decades have witnessed a great rise in the number of interest groups, especially in Washington, and there are many charges of extreme interest influence in Washington. All of this coincides with arguments of the decline of the parties. Also important to note is that the equations seem to indicate that even though parties may have some effects on economic growth, their effects are completely overwhelmed by the influence of interest groups. In the face of strong interests, the current American parties may indeed be weak, and may not be strong enough to be encompassing interests, as Olson suggested.

CONCLUSIONS

We have attempted to build a stronger test of Olson's interest group theory of economic stagnation than previously offered in the literature. Refinements were offered in terms of the measurement of the key variable: interest group strength. Special attention was paid to the dynamic quality of the theory and the need to measure interest group strength over time. Further, Olson's model was tested against a major competitor: the party model. Such a model was integrated into Olson's broad theoretical outline by conceptualizing parties as potential encompassing interests. Comparative American state data were used to test the interest group and party models. While the interest group variables remained in the final equation, party, measured as changing levels of party competition, was found not to be significant when controlling for the effects of interests. Because of the potential theoretical interest of parties, more and better measures of the strength of the party system

need to be developed. Finally, the measurement critique
of Olson bore fruit as the predicted power of the interest group model was shown to be far superior to the results that Olson found.

These results also have implications for economic
growth policies. Insofar as a nation's policies allow
the growth and proliferation of interest groups, its
economic health may suffer. However, the costs of lost
personal freedom, a foundation for modern representative democracies, if policies that would restrict interest groups are developed, may be too great to consider.
Again, one sees the tension between economics and freedom that modern representative democracies must try to
balance. From this, one can also see the inherent in-
stability of democracies and the possible implications
of economic and industrial policy on the future political stability of the Western democratic world.

NOTES

1. But Chamberlain (1974) argues that, under some
conditions, individuals will contribute to large groups.
2. These figures are taken from the Statistical
Abstract of the United States.
3. Olson also raises this question (1982, p. 106).
4. Here I should note that Olson's requirements
for parties to be encompassing interests resembles the
requirements of the responsible parties doctrine.
5. The sources for the data are Ranney (1971) and
Bibby (1980).
6. I have excluded Alaska from these calculations
because Alaska shows growth at levels much beyond the
number two state, Wyoming. The figures are 15.5 percent
for Alaska and 7.1 percent for Wyoming. The average
state saw growth of about 4.0 percent.

6
Industrial Democracy in Europe and the Prospects for Industrial Policy

Anton Pelinka

Industrial democracy, developed and implemented mainly in Europe, is a concept which includes a variety of models providing for the participation of employees or their representatives in the decision making process within corporations and/or within the national economy. Industrial democracy is a conceptual challenge to the traditional rules of Western society; its basic premise is that workers should be accepted as partners in decision making by owners. Labor must balance capital. Industrial democracy does not liquidate private ownership; it stays within the framework of a capitalist society since it is built upon the recognition of privately owned industry of private capital (IRG, 1981; Roberts, 1979).

Industrial democracy was designed as a third way between the traditional market economy and centrally planned economy and between the monopolies of private ownership and collective ownership. As a "third way" concept, it has been put forth by Social Democrats (Pelinka, 1983, pp. 134-37), and, to a lesser extent, by Christian Democrats and Conservatives. Norway is an example of the ideological variability of industrial democracy. The Conservative Party, now ruling for some years, proclaims in its 1981 party manifesto "Economic Democracy" as the party's official goal (Lafferty, 1984). The Norwegian Conservatives, for instance, understand economic democracy to be a program for expanded employee stock ownership, i.e., codetermination by coownership.

The European People's Party, the umbrella organization of Christian Democratic Parties within the European Community, openly favors industrial democracy (Aughey & Rizzuto, 1984). These are only a few examples of not only the variety of ideological traditions claiming responsibility for "economic" or "industrial" democracy but also the variety of interpretations this concept permits.

A Scandinavian political party, the Swedish Social Democratic Labor Party, developed a clear distinction between the different levels of industrial and economic democracy. Starting from below, it declares workers' codetermination on the plant-level (working place democracy), on the collective bargaining level, and on the managerial level as industrial democracy. Financial participation is a concept of the Swedish Social Democrats called the "Meidner Plan" (Elvander, 1979, pp. 152-54)--participation in decision making on the managerial level as in nation-wide planning. This is economic democracy.

The distinction between industrial democracy and economic democracy is that industrial democracy is on the corporate level and economic democracy is above the corporate level. Industrial democracy on the corporate level is linked with the idea of direct workers' participation; economic democracy is linked with the idea of neocorporatism, power-sharing between government, labor (represented by unions), and capital (represented by employers' associations) (Schmitter & Lehmbruch, 1979).

To analyze economic democracy, the role unions play in industrial democracy must first be analyzed. Which unions are tempted to follow the strategy toward economic democracy and why? Which unions are more skeptical concerning this neocorporatist understanding of industrial democracy?

Neocorporatism is to be understood as the construction of tripartism within the framework of liberal systems of competitive party system and capitalism (Lehmbruch & Schmitter, 1982). Neocorporatism means the liberalization and democratization of corporatism. It is not the antithesis of parliamentary rule. It is a decisive supplement aimed at the integration of industrial relations into the political system. It is industrial

TABLE 6.1
THE CONCEPT OF ECONOMIC AND INDUSTRIAL DEMOCRACY
ACCORDING TO THE SWEDISH SOCIAL DEMOCRATIC LABOR
PARTY

A. PUBLIC ECONOMIC PLANNING

B. FINANCIAL PARTICIPATION
    Wage Earners' Investment
    Funds

C. CODETERMINATION: WORKERS
    ON BOARDS
    Laws on Representation of
    Employees on the Boards
    of Private Companies and   Economic
    Public Agencies   Democracy

D. COLLECTIVE BARGAINING   Industrial
    The Codetermination Act   Democracy
    (MBL)

E. SHOP FLOOR PARTICIPATION
    The Act Concerning the
    Status of the Shop Stewards;
    The Worker Protection Act;
    The Work Environment Act

Source: Erik Asard, "Industrial and Economic
         Democracy in Sweden: From Consensus to
         Confrontation," Paper presented to the
         Workshop on Industrial Democracy, ECPR,
         Salzburg, 1984.

democracy (Levinson, 1974) but democracy on a very
centralized level; democracy as codetermination
at the top. The main democratic quality can be
seen in the participation of the majority. The
participation of labor is the reason why neocorporatism can be called a contribution to the development of liberal democracy. In this respect,
the organization of labor again is an important
variable.
    Two hypotheses shall be discussed:
    -The organization of unions determines the
     development of economic democracy directly

by influencing the leading interest of one
of the main actors. Neocorporatism is con-
stituted by the interest of the elite speaking for labor.
-The organization of unions determines the
development of neocorporatism indirectly by
influencing the social perception of those
who are necessary to legitimate neocorpor-
tism, the people who have to accept process
and outcomes of neocorporatism, at least in
principle.

THE PLAUSIBILITY OF THE HYPOTHESES

Philippe C. Schmitter (1979) presented eight criteria that produce a framework favorable for industrial democracy (p. 66 ff.). These criteria
may depend on the organization and structure of
unions:

Limited number: The smaller the number of
neocorporatist agents, the better the ability
of a neocorporatist system to develop, adapt,
and survive. The perfect number would be
three: one agent speaking for each of the
three partners. If a certain union movement
allows representation by only one agent,
that is, if a certain union movement is
centralized as extreme as possible, neocorporatism is backed by a favorable condition.
Singular: The singularity of the union movement integrated into the system of industrial
democracy is a favorable condition as well,
a variation of the criterion mentioned above.
Compulsory: The output of neocorporatist decision making should be as obligatory as possible. A union participating within the
"black box" of the political system facili-
tates the compulsory character of decisions.
The integration of unions in the center of
the political system is one more favorable
condition.
Neocompetitive: "Social peace" is influenced
by the development of cooperative union policies. The strategic orientation of unions
has its impact on the degree of competitiveness.

<u>Hierarchically ordered</u>: Decision making from above is an impact of centralization; the centralization of unions is again important.
<u>Functionally differentiated</u>: Unions that are able to abstain from an antagonistic approach, i.e., unions accepting a balanced as well as permanent role that capital and its representatives have to play, are important for the tripartite balance on which industrial democracy has to rely.
<u>Recognition by state</u>: The integration of unions, their merger with the state, permits the fulfillment of that condition.
<u>Representational monopoly</u>: A union movement, comprehending all the different ideological traditions and status interests labor consists of, creates and institutionalizes monopoly on one side and favors monopolies on the other (on government and on capital).

European unions can be described in different ways (Kendall, 1975; Mielke, 1983). To demonstrate the possible correlation between unions and neocorporatism, the following typology will be used (Von Beyme, 1980, pp. 146-206).

- ideological orientation
- strategic orientation
- degree of organization
- degree of centralization

IDEOLOGICAL ORIENTATION

Ideological orientation can be measured by the distance unions are from society and government (Von Beyme, 1980, pp. 293-301). According to this approach, unions can be either opposition or reformist in nature. Opposition unions are influenced more or less by a Maxist view of society. The political instruments they favor are mostly the classical instruments of Marxism, aiming at the socialization of the means of production. Opposition unions are communist-influenced unions such as the French CGT and the Portuguese CGTP-IN or, to a lesser extent, the Italian CGIL. The British TUC, not at all based on Marxist-Leninist tradition, can be called an opposition union as well. It is the only example of social democratic union confederation which tends to oppose the economic subsystem in principle (Dorfmann, 1979).

Reformist unions are most of the Social Democratic and all the Christian Democratic unions. Their goal is to improve the present social and economic conditions of workers. Their instruments are those of a welfare state.

Not all unions fit clearly into these two patterns--the French CFDT, for instance, originally a Christian Democratic union, now much more a lfeftist Social Democratic union, seems to be somewhere in between. The model of socialism by self-administration of the workers that the CFDT is promoting is neither a traditional Marxist nor a pure reformist model (Von Beyme, 1980, pp. 295-98).

Industrial democracy asks for a balanced recognition of capital by labor and vice versa. Opposition unions do not accept the legitimacy of capital, at least not in the long run. The neocorporatist triangle is anathema for them, acceptable only perhaps for a transition period but not as a permanently established decision making pattern. So the expectation is that there should be a significant correlation between the degree of reformist ideological orientation and a union's inclination for neocorporatism.

Strategic Organization

Ideological orientation obviously is linked to strategic orientation. Strategic orientation is measured by short-term behavior of unions on questions such as wage policy and strike activity as well as by long-term behavior including social confrontation or social integration. The conflict orientation indicates the union's principal strategic orientation. Conflict orientation is the result of internal and external factors consisting of the impact of the organization of the union itself and of the strategic orientation that the union's opponents have--the employers and their organization (Von Beyme, 1980, pp. 168-72).

High strike frequency stands for conflict orientation and for nonintegration (or a low level of integration) into the political system. Neocorporatism is the integration of unions par excellence. A low degree of conflict orientation is probably the consequence of a strategic orien-

tation which includes participation in a network
of industrial democracy. The data from the International Labor Organization (1983, pp. 42f) reveal
most of the Scandinavian union movements (the exception is Finland), the Swiss, the Austrian, and
the German unions (and to a lesser extent the
Dutch unions) are examples of a strategic orientation which implies union participation. All these
unions act in a very cooperative way--their strike
frequency is, for a long period, significantly low.

Degree of Organization

Organization can be measured by comparing membership density (Mielke, 1983; Von Beyme, 1980, pp.
75-77). Membership density differs strongly
across European union movements. About one third
of the labor force is organized in France, Spain,
and Switzerland. The reason for this is the weakness the political left showed for a long period
(as in France up to 1981), the unbroken tradition
of pure capitalism, and, in the case of Spain, the
lack of union freedom until 1976.

On the other end are countries--led by Sweden,
Belgium, Austria, and Ireland--where membership
density is significantly higher than 50 percent;
in Sweden it is above the 80 percent mark. German,
Italian, British, and Dutch union federations are
in between; their membership density is about 40
percent or a little more. According to the newest
data, Greek as well as Portuguese union federations
belong to this middle group (Mielke, 1983, pp. 483-
93, 922-28). The Greek and the Portuguese organizations indicate that the delay of union freedom
does not necessarily imply low membership density.

It can be assumed that an increase in membership density pushes the inclination of unions toward an acceptance of industrial democracy. Unions
organized more completely are not obliged to win
a majority of the labor force; they still represent labor. They are not bound permanently to
prove their ability to promote the interests of
the workers. Highly organized unions seem to
start and to institutionalize a bargain with the
other side.

Degree of Centralization

Centralization has to be observed on two different
levels: the question of integration of all unions
in one national confederation; and the question of
the division of intraunion decision making power
between the institution on the top and the institutions below.

Decentralization on the first level can be
the result of ideological differences. That is
the case in France, Italy, Spain, Portugal, Belgium, Switzerland, the Netherlands, and Greece.
Decentralization can be also the result of social
differences--in spite of existing national confederations, white collar unions are not integrated in the nationwide umbrella organizations in
Germany, Sweden, Denmark, and Finland. In Italy
as well as in the Netherlands, there has been the
experiment of national platforms built in the
1970s to start an association of the different,
ideologically separated unions. The process aimed
at central confederations seems not yet finished
(Mielke, 1983, pp. 596-616, 820-33).

Intraunion centralization can be analyzed in
two cases: the British TUC is an example of a
national confederation integrating different unions,
enjoying a monopoly on the national level, but an
organization characterized by its lack of central
authority (Dorfmann, 1979). The Austrian OëGB is
the opposite case--a perfect national monopoly
combined with a highly developed and well established authority for the confederation's leadership (Pelinka, 1980).

As neocorporatism is based on elitist and exclusive cooperation between a number of representatives as small as possible, centralization as a
method of reducing the number of decision makers
seems to fit perfectly into tripartism. A positive correlation between union centralization and
industrial democracy is very plausible.

A HYPOTHETICAL TYPOLOGY OF UNION TENDENCES
TOWARD NEOCORPORATISM

Some of the criteria used for the typology above
are easily translated in empirical data: strike
frequency as an indicator for strategic orienta-

tion and membership density as an indicator for the degree of organization. Ideological orientation can be added insofar as membership in the communist-oriented World Federation of Trade Unions (WFTU) of one of the large national confederations (like the French CGT) can be interpreted as a tendency in the direction of "opposition unions." Degree of centralization can be operationalized at least one one level: Is there a monopolistic national confederation?

The basic assumptions made above lead to particular indicators. A union movement inclined to accept the invitation for participation in a neocorporatist set-up has the following characteristics:

1. strike frequency significantly below the average, very probably below 50 strike minutes per employee per year;
2. membership density significantly above the average, very probably about 60 or more percent employees organized;
3. ideological link with reformism expressed in an undisputed organizational link with the Social Democratic International Confederation Trade Unions (ICFU) or the Christian Democratic World Confederation of Labor (WCL);
4. perfect or almost perfect monopoly of one national confederation integrating different ideological traditions as well as different status interests.

All four of these conditions are met clearly by the Norwegian LO and by the Austrian OëGB. In both cases, only condition 2 is not fulfilled perfectly. Both union confederations have a membership density between 50 and 60 (above the average but not top ranking). None of these conditions are fulfilled in France; the French union movement is an example for organized labor far away from all the criteria permitting neocorporatism (see Table 6.2).

The other European unions are more or less between these extreme types. The Swedish unions, for instance, lean much more to the neocorporatist type--only the existence of white-collar TCO besides the national confederation LO and the extreme strike activity in one year, 1980, completely

TABLE 6.2
CONDITIONS FAVORABLE FOR "INDUSTRIAL DEMOCRACY" ABOVE CORPORATE LEVEL

Country	Strike Frequency[a]	Membership Density[b]	Ideological Linkage[c]	Monopolistic Degree[d]	Degree of inclination to neocorporatism
Austria	2	2	2	2	8
Belgium	1	2	2	0	5
Denmark	1	2	2	1	6
Finland	1	2	2	1	6
France	1	0	0	0	1
Germany	2	1	2	1	6
Great Britain	0	1	2	2	5
Ireland	0	2	2	2	6
Italy	0	1	1	1	3
Netherlands	2	1	2	1	6
Norway	2	2	2	2	8
Portugal	?	1	0	0	?
Spain	0	1	2	0	3
Sweden	1	2	2	1	6
Switzerland	2	0	2	0	4

a - 0=above 200; 1=about average; 2=below 50.
b - 0=below one third; 1=about average; 2=above one half.
c - 0=mainly WFTU; 1=partly WFTU; 2=none WFTU.
d - 0=fragmentation; 1=almost monopoly; 2=perfect monopoly.

untypical for the last decades, prohibit the place-
ment of Sweden with Norway and Austria. Italian
labor tends, as another example, much more to the
French position; but a higher membership density
and the first step in the direction to establish
an integrated national confederation differenti-
ate France and Italy.

British and Irish labor are deviant cases.
Both the British TUC and the Irish ICTU have a
monopoly as national confederations, both are
linked with the ICFU, both have a membership density at least not below the average, but both have
a strike frequency dramatically above the European
average. The correlations between strike frequency and membership density does not exist in the
British and Irish cases (see Table 6.2).

To explain these deviations, historical and
political backgrounds have to be considered (Kendall, 1975). In Britain and Ireland, the labor
movement has been established as a union movement
first--the Labour Party was an organizational
latecomer. In both countries, unions are, despite
the monopoly the confederations enjoy, very decentralized. In both union movements, intraunion democracy is defined as grassroots participation--
much more so than on the continent.

The deviant cases of Britain and Ireland demonstrate the prize neocorporatist inclination has
for unions. It is a prize which has to be paid in
intraunion democracy: neocorporatism is a pattern
for the active participation of a few. The role
the many have to play is reduced to acclamation.

Of course, union structures are developing as
are neocorporatist structures. There are many
factors which may change the European scene. The
successes of socialist and social democratic parties in the Mediterranean countries in the 1980s
will have some impact on industrial relations as
will the defeats of socialists and social democrats in their traditional strongholds in western,
northern, and central Europe (Pelinka, 1983).
Other events influence union organizations and
strategies and industrial democracy as a concept
as well as a reality.

There is no industrial democracy without the
participation of unions; and, there is no participation of unions without their integration into

the political system, into the established political, social, and economic order. The entry of unions into the "black box," the power center of the liberal systems, is an unconditional necessity for the development of neocorporatism as industrial democracy from above. A necessary precondition is the reconciliation of organized labor and the system.

TWO CASE STUDIES

Neocorporatism as industrial democracy requires participation of labor by unions, but industrial democracy has to have its second part--direct participation of labor by the employees themselves. On the corporate level, industrial democracy relates to individuals (the employees) or their shop stewards which in most of the European countries are usually closely linked with unions. But they do not represent, at least theoretically, the unions on the corporate level, but the workers within the unions.

To analyze industrial democracy on the corporate level, a brief overview will be given about two cases which differ significantly, but which demonstrate the variety of European developments: Great Britain is an example of the reversal of a trend toward industrial democracy, a country which lacks industrial democracy; and Sweden is still the model for industrial democracy as an overall concept, especially after the renewal of social democratic dominance in 1982, a country balancing centralized and decentralized industrial democracy.

Great Britain

Great Britain's industrial relations have always been strongly influenced by its large number of unions. Despite a long-term process of amalgamation reducing the number of unions, especially pure craft unions, the heterogeneity is still strong enough to prevent a central strategy to establish industrial democracy. The failure of the Labour government between 1974 and 1979 to establish a kind of continental and EC-influenced determination seems to be a significant factor

(Gourevitch et al., 1984, pp. 13-88; Roberts, 1979, pp. 164-69).

The British situation after 1945 was characterized by the decisive position the shop stewards' committees had in the collective bargaining process. The shop stewards tried to exploit the possibilities to get special improvements for the workers they were representing: improvements in pay and terms of employment superior to the results settled at the level of industry by unions and employers' associations. So the British situation was characterized by decentralization instead of centralization, more direct and less indirect participation, but also unofficial strikes against bargains on the corporate level.

In 1965, the Labour government appointed a Royal Commission of Trade Unions and Employers' Association. The Commission declared the British system of industrial relations dysfunctional-- disintegrated the collective bargaining system into two systems, one on the centralized level of industry and the other on the decentralized level of corporations and plants; and created a permanent conflict which was responsible for the decline of the TUC and the ability to adapt British industry to new challenges.

The diagnosis was clear, but the remedy was disputed. There was no consequence under Labour, but changes were made under the incoming Conservative government. The Conservatives introduced in 1971 the Industrial Relations Act which was never accepted by the unions and was repealed when the Labour government returned to power in 1974. The Labour Party and the unions especially opposed the legal liability of unions. But the Labour government officially announced its interest in an improvement of industrial relations; and in 1975, the "Committee on Industrial Democracy and Proposed Legislation" (better known as the Bullock Committee after its chairman) started to work.

The committee's results aimed clearly to Europeanize British industrial relations. Following the German concept of codetermination, the majority of the Bullock Committee endorsed the principle of employee representation on the board, a kind of parity codetermination after the model of the German Montan codetermination (Gourevitch

et al., 1984, pp. 89-188). The Bullock proposal
faced opposition from all sides. The employers
declared it was the beginning of socialism and
the pereptuation of class war within the corporations, but some unions announced that they were
not willing to participate and be integrated into
a capitalist system. The Labour government rejected some of the Bullock Committee proposals
and in the government's "White Paper on Industrial
Democracy" explained the lines it intended to follow after the elections of 1979. But Labour lost,
and the specific concept of codetermination lost
too. Due to the bitter confrontation between the
Conservative government and the unions (Gourevitch
et al., 1984, pp. 64-69), there is little chance
in the near future of a new step toward industrial democracy. Britain will stay British, deeply
fragmented between two subsocieties, with a high
level of industrial conflict and lacking industrial democracy.

Sweden

Sweden has been regarded as a model for other industrial countries for decades. Based on the ex-
ceptional degree of unionization, almost 90 percent, collective bargaining became more and more
centralized and carried on at the national level.
Economic considerations, political loyalties toward the social democratic government, and a
solidaristic wage policy were the main reasons
for this centralization. It has to be stressed
that the Swedish Employers' Association (SAF) was
at least as anxious as the leading trade union
federation, LO, to introduce more and more central agreements not allowing a wage policy re-
specting regional or sectoral differences (Elvander, 1979, pp. 130-45).

This centralization has to be seen in combin-
ation with a delayed but now highly developed employee participation. In the 1970s, participation
on the corporate level, in the sense of codetermination, became a leading issue in Swedish politics. Already in 1946, works councils had been
established as joint institutions for cooperation
between employers and employees, institutions on
the corporate level, not unlike the Austrian Joint

Commission on Wages and Prices founded in 1957 on the national level (Pelinka, 1981).

The works councils seemed to be enough to satisfy the need for industrial democracy on the corporate level. But by the end of the 1960s, the works councils became increasingly criticized for their restrictions of achieving the best possible production. The works councils did not really establish parity in power. In 1970 and 1971, the TCO, the white-collar union outside the LO, as well as the LO itself, started a political campaign demanding new legislation to implement a better developed codetermination. This campaign resulted in the Codetermination Act, passed by the parliament in 1976 immediately before the Social Democrats lost the general elections and the center right coalition came into power for six years. The Codetermination Act strengthened considerably the position of employees: allotment and supervision of work, personnel management, and work environment now became open to negotiations between management and employees. Already in 1972 and 1974, employees' representation on the board was established but below parity and not following the parity rule known only by the German Montan codetermination which ruled the steel and coal industry.

The electoral defeat of the Social Democrats resulted partly from the Meidner Report which declared collective capital formation. Wage Earners' Investment Funds financed to a certain degree by private owners, as an official goal of the Social Democratic Labor Party as well as of the LO (Gourevitch et al., 1984, pp. 272-75). After 1982 the hard core of the Meidner Report came on the agenda again as a possible step toward an overall economic democracy.

This comparison between the economic and the social performance of Great Britain and Sweden reveals significant differences. Great Britain is undoubtedly the economic loser among European nations. For decades now, economic indicators have demonstrated the decline of Britain as an industrial power: per capita income went down compared with the OECD average; productivity did the same; and unemployment and frequency of strikes are

always above the European average. On the other
side, Sweden--one of the leading earlier European
industrial nations--was always among the leading
group in productivity and per capita income.
Swedish unemployment and strike frequency was usually below the European average as well.

Of course, these examples must not be simpli-
fied as the consequence of industrial democracy
alone. There are many reasons for Britain's economic downfall, but one can conclusively say that
industrial democracy did not prevent economic efficiency or that industrial democracy can result
from and stimulate a successful industrial policy.
Whoever thinks there is a contradiction or at
least a tension between an efficient industrial
policy and an established industrial democracy
should analyze the European reality (IRG, 1981,
p. 334f).

FUTURE PERSPECTIVES OF INDUSTRIAL
DEMOCRACY IN EUROPE

Because there is no European industrial democracy
but only industrial democracy in different European countries, a Europeanization of industrial
democracy to include not just the EC but all of
Europe is still the goal of the future. There is
no European standard, but there could be one.
What has been established within the EC as the
Council for Economic and Social Affairs is just a
beginning of centralized European industrial democracy; what has been advised by the EC as a model
for codetermination on the corporate level, a
powersharing of labor below parity, is just the
first step (Von Beyme, 1980, pp. 294-301). The
foundation of the European Trade Union Confederation, including all national noncommunist union
federations and the Italian CGIL, but not the
French CGT (Von Beyme, 1980, pp. 27f.), is just
the creation of the possibility of further efforts
to establish a balance between transnational capital organized by multinational corporations and
transnational labor organized by multinational
unions.

Industrial democracy is still seeking balance
between codetermination on the national level,
i.e., neocorporatism, and codetermination on the

corporate level. Austria may be an example for a
lack of balance, for too much centralization of
industrial democracy (Gourevitch et al., 1984,
pp. 70-73; Von Beyme, 1980, pp. 295-98). Sweden
seems to be a better example for a system emphasiz-
ing both the national level to guarantee economi-
clly reasonable and socially solidaristic policies
and the corporate (or plant) level to guarantee
more than a minimum of direct participation in industrial democracy.

Industrial democracy must still be defended
on two fronts. On the one side, most of the com-
munist unions (with the exception of the Italian
and Spanish communists) still defame industrial
democracy as a sly invention of sophisticated
capitalism to restrain labor from successful class
warfare; and some trend within noncommunist left-
ist unions, like within the French CFDT or the
British TUC, are still opposed to the consequences
of industrial democracy, shared responsibility resulting from shared power (Pelinka, 1981). On
the other side, traditional employers and traditional economists resent industrial democracy as
a violation of the market's rules and as a step
toward political interference into business. Industrial democracy has to prove its ability to
reform gradually, within the rules of pluralism
and of liberal democracy but, nevertheless, reform that includes a tendency toward mixed economy and a democracy centered not only on the political system but on the society as a whole.

7
The Future of Industrial Policy: Conclusion

Steven A. Shull

Public concern for industrial policies seems to arise with bad economic conditions. As a result, these policies are frequently based on piecemeal decisions rather than on long-range planning. This is particularly true in the United States where there has been little agreement on what the problems are and even less on what the solutions should be. Economists often oppose industrial policies as government intervention because they tend to favor the market to solve economic problems. The main thesis of this volume is that politics is the most important reason for the occurrence and type of industrial policy or the lack thereof. The difficult decision for government to intervene is primarily political and based upon a host of conditions including political culture and ideology, the context of interactions by governmental and nongovernmental institutions, and the content of policy itself. The remainder of this conclusion summarizes the interpretations drawn from the contributors with a particular eye for the prospects of an industrial policy in the United States.

When comparing industrial policy in Europe and the United States, considerable similarities and differences emerge. There seems greater commitment and agreement for government intervention in the former to cure societal woes. Redistributive policies are more easily formulated in Europe than in the United States which offers lower levels of social guarantees. And yet, Europe in the

1980s seems to be placing greater emphasis on economic than social policies. Lawrence believes that the United States has a more flexible economy than most of the European nations and, therefore, may need better targeting for those policies it chooses to adopt. At the same time, generally, there is less consensus in the United States for what such policies should encompass. Thus, despite similarities of economic problems between the United States and Europe, solutions to them probably will not be the same.

We have referred to Europe as if it were a single entity, but it is clear that except most recently for steel, there is little industrial policy for Europe as a whole. Lauber explored several reasons for this phenomena including conflicting interests, ideology, nationalism, limited resources, and legal restrictions on the powers of the European Community (EC). He believes that the potential for more cooperative policies exists, however, and states: "It seems possible that in the changed environment, an affirmative industrial policy of the European Community might yet develop." Lauber pointed to several promising examples of greater European cooperation, such as a model code for national subsidies and rules on government transfer of payments.

Pelinka also referred to the lack of an industrial policy in Europe as a whole. There is no European standard, but he believes that there could be one. He contends that in individual countries, at least, his ideal of "industrial democracy can result from and stimulate a successful industrial policy." He points to Sweden as the best example of this ideal but states that, to be successful, industrial democracy will have to be "a reform which includes a tendency toward mixed economy and a democracy centered not only on the political system but on the society as a whole."

The American political context is a very different one, even though all Western societies are influenced by the mix of domestic, international, and economic policies in their politics. Still, the neocorporatism discussed by Pelinka in several countries of Europe (particularly smaller ones like Norway and Austria) is much less likely in

the United States. Both of the papers dealing
with American politics gave major attention to
the segmented nature of American politics and
public policy. Cohen and Brunk show that the
American industrial complex has been suffering
for over a decade with massive trade deficits and
declining jobs and productivity. Still, they and
Peters believe that a comprehensive industrial
policy is not economically desirable or politically feasible in the United States. A comprehensive industrial policy might be more desirable
if the United States were a more corporatist and
centralized society, but the obstacles are many.

What are the major industrial and trade problems America faces and are they subject to solution by government? Conservative Kevin Phillips
(1984) states that "too many dollars spent by
U.S. consumers are stimulating jobs in Asia rather
than Alabama" (p. 22). It is also true that American productivity levels have risen as fast as
in Japan and the emerging industrial nations of
East Asia. The Presidential Commission on Industrial Competitiveness (1985) states that Japan
has five times America's overall productivity
rate. It also points to the problems of high
cost capital investment, high wage and monetary
exchange rates, and inconsistent trade laws. Virtually all writers agree that the federal deficit
must be reduced.

It is easier to agree on what America's industrial problems are than it is to agree on what
the solutions should be. The Presidential Commission made ninety recommendations including two
new Cabinet-level departments for science and
technology. Phillips (1984) wants an expanded
import-export bank, liberalized antitrust laws,
and generally a more pro-business climate. Dolbeare (1984) asserts that there can be "no economic revival without political revival" (p. xii).
He believes that we "have a rare opportunity to
preserve and enhance the democratic essence of
our society" (p. xiii).

Lawrence is skeptical about whether the
United States can or should have an industrial
policy. He views many of America's economic problems as macroeconomic in nature but, for reasons
above, thinks they are not capable of solution by

comprehensive government policy. However, he believes that we need a more broadly available research and development policy and more investment
in training and education.

While none of the contributors believe that
comprehensive industrial policy is required in
America, several are of the opinion that social
policies such as retraining and relocation might
be desirable. We have seen that the establishment
of an industrial policy for the United States is
a very controversial question. It would involve
achieving a consensus among different industries,
organized labor, and government regarding the objectives of such a policy and the methods of its
implementation. Objections are likely to be
raised on ideological, economic, social, and political grounds. The "ideal" of nonintervention
by government in the economy (regulation or de-
regulation) would be brought up; and politicians
may fear that the establishment of an industrial
policy might reduce opportunities for providing
favors to important constituents and hurt their
chances for reelection.

Proponents argue that an ideal industrial
policy could have very important humanitarian advantages. It could moderate the volatile swings
of the economy and provide greater income predic-
tability for Americans. This, in turn, could enhance the quality of life in the United States
since employment opportunities would stabilize and
become more predictable. With tax revenues also
becoming more predictable over the long haul, educational and cultural institutions would benefit.

A full industrial policy would be committed
to restructure basic U.S. industries to enable
them to take their place as healthy competitors
in the world markets and to maintain the United
States as a country in which all geographical
areas (and thereby all classes and races) share
the burden as well as the benefits which this
country has to offer. Such a policy is unlikely
in the United States because it would require
greater cooperation and coordination between industry, labor, and government than has existed
heretofore. Investment would need to be stimu-
lated in "sunrise" industries, and the pain of
disinvestment eased in "sunset" industries (Baker,

1984; Thayer, 1984). Conflicting interests must
be reconciled; retraining programs may be needed
on a massive scale, but workers' productivity
must be enhanced in order to maintain the international competitiveness of plants and industries
(Presidential Commission, 1985). These conditions
seem unlikely in the immediate future. Whether
the United States has a formal policy or not, its
ability to export must be increased if it is to
continue to function as a flourishing democracy
worthy of emulation (Adams & Behrman, 1982; Dolbeare, 1984).

But an effective industrial policy would have
to recognize and cushion the social shocks inevitably created by the process of adjusting to changing technological and international conditions.
Such a policy requires a management that would
keep in mind the improvement of the quality of
life of all Americans. As Felix G. Rohatyn (1983)
has said:

> America cannot survive half rich, half poor,
> half suburb, half slum. If the country soon
> wakes up, it will not do so by way of lais-
> sez faire; nor will it do so by way of the
> old liberalism which has proven itself in-
> capable of coping with our present problems.
> It will do so only by building a mixed eco-
> nomy, geared mostly to business enterprises
> in which an active partnership between busi-
> ness, labor, and government strikes the kind
> of bargains--whether on an energy policy,
> regional policy or industrial policy--that
> an advanced Western democracy requires to
> function and that, in one form or another,
> have been made for years in Europe and Japan.
> This partnership will have to be as indige-
> nous to our culture and traditions as those
> of Germans and Japanese have been to theirs,
> and it will have to be competitive (p. 137).

Questions of trade relate to the performance of
American industry. Current concerns about productivity and declining competitiveness in certain
areas have given great impetus to the discussion
of industrial policy (one bibliography provides
950 sources on the topic; Harwood, 1985). Whether
one backs failing industries or attempts to pick

winners, it remains highly controversial. But industrial policy is also likely to become increasingly important as decision makers confront the limitations of traditional fiscal and monetary policies. Its strengths and weaknesses must be faced squarely because no country's industrial policy is yet (or likely to be) a panacea for economic disruptions or decline.

Proponents of an industrial policy argue that a nation that casually surrenders leading industrial positions through policies of neglect (or no policies at all) will find it difficult to stage a comeback, particularly if it falls into long periods of noncompetitiveness. They assert that a cluster of strategies is needed to reverse this decline. We believe that forums of discussion among representatives of governmental institutions and economic forces, such as this one, can help develop such strategies. Above all, the creation of industrial policies must be based on an educational process including a sharing of information through which we can learn about the problems of others and how all can mutually interact to solve these joint problems. While the contributors to this volume are not optimistic about the feasibility of a comprehensive industrial policy for the United States, they have made us aware of the economic and political problems that ensue from the world's increasing interdependence.

Bibliography

Adams, F. Gerald, and Jere R. Behrman (eds.)(1982).
    Commodity Exports and Economic Development
    (Lexington, Mass.: D.C. Heath).
American Iron and Steel Institute (1981). Steel
    at the Crossroad: One Year Later (Washington,
    D.C.: AISI).
American Iron and Steel Institute (1983). Surging
    Unfair Trade for Developing Countries: An
    Old Problem with New Faces (Washington, D.C.:
    AISI).
Anderson, James E., David W. Brady, Charles S.
    Bullock, III, and Joseph Stewart, Jr. (1984).
    Public Policy-Making, 3rd ed. (New York: Holt,
    Rinehart, and Winston).
Asard, Erik (1984). "Industrial and Economic Demo-
    cracy in Sweden: From Consensus to Confronta-
    tion," Paper presented to the Workshop on In-
    dustrial Democracy, ECPR, Salzburg.
Aughey, A., and F.P. Rizzuto (1984). "The Emergence
    of Conservative/Christian Democratic Consensus
    on the Rights for Morkers in TNC's," Paper pre-
    sented to the Workshop on Industrial Democracy,
    ECPR, Salzburg.
Badaracco, J.L., and D.B. Yoffie (1983). "Industri-
    al Policy: It Can't Happen Here," Harvard
    Business Review (November/December), pp. 97-
    105.
Barker, Michael (ed.) (1984). Rebuilding America's
    Infrastructure (Durham, N.C.: Duke University
    Press).

Baumer, Donald C., and Carl E. Van Horn (1985).
The Politics of Unemployment (Washington,
D.C.: Congressional Quarterly Press).

Bibby, John F., Cornelius C. Cotter, James L.
Gibson, and Robert J. Huckshorn (1980).
"Parties in State Politics" in Politics in
the American States: A Comparative Analysis,
edited by Virginia Gray, Herbert Jacob, and
Kenneth Vines, 4th ed. (Boston: Little,
Brown).

Bluestone, B. (1985). "Comments on Do We Need
an Industrial Policy?" Harpers (February),
pp. 35-48.

Blumenthal, W. Michael (1978). "Steering in
Crowded Waters," Foreign Affairs 56 (July):
728-39.

Bosworth, B.P. (1984). Tax Incentives and Economic Growth (Washington, D.C.: The Brookings
Institution).

Calleo, David P., and Benjamin M. Rowland (1973).
America and the World Political Economy
(Bloomington, Ind.: Indiana University Press).

Chamberlain, John (1974). "Provision of Collective
Goods as a Function of Group Size," American
Political Science Review 68 (September):707-
15.

Choi, Kwang (1983). "A Statistical Test of Olson's
Model," in The Political Economy of Growth,
edited by D. Mueller (New Haven: Yale University Press).

Choate, P., and S. Walter (1981). America in
Ruins: Beyond the Public Works Pork Barrel
(Washington, D.C.: Council of State Planning
Agencies).

Cohen, J.E. (1985). "Interest Groups, Parties and
Economic Growth in the American States,"
Paper prepared for Symposium on Economics
and Politics of Industrial Policy, University of New Orleans, New Orleans, La., February 21-22.

Conjuncture (1985). (Paris: Paribus).

Connerly, Charles E. (1983). "Industrial Policy:
Conservative, Liberal and Radical Views,"
Policy Studies Journal 12 (December):390-94.

Council on Economic Priorities (1981). The Iron
Triangle (New York: CEP).

Cronin, Thomas E. (1970). "Everybody Believes in Democracy Until He Gets to the White House: An Examination of White House-Departmental Relations," Law and Contemporary Problems 35: 573-625.

Curzon-Price, Victoria (1981). Industrial Policy in the European Community (London: Macmillan Trade Policy Research Center).

Davignon, Etienne (1984). Berichte und Informationen. Bonn: Press and Information Office, European Community (July 3, September 18, November 12, December 18).

Defreigne, Pierre (1984). "Towards Concerted-Industrial Policies in the EC," in European Industry: Public Policy and Corporate Strategy, edited by Alexis Jacquemin (Oxford: Clarendon Press).

Denzau, Arthur T. (1983). "Will an 'Industrial Policy' Work for the United States?" (St. Louis: Washington University Center for the Study of American Business, Vol. 57, September, p. 3).

deLettenhove, Albert Kervin (1984). "Steel: A Case Study" in European Industry: Public Policy and Corporate Strategy, edited by Alexis Jacquemin (Oxford: Clarendon Press).

Dolbeare, Kenneth M. (1982). American Public Policy: A Citizen's Guide (New York: McGraw-Hill).

Dolbeare, Kenneth M. (1984). Democracy at Risk: Politics of Economic Renewal (Chatham, N.J.: Chatham House).

Dorfmann, Gerald A. (1979). Government Versus Trade Unionism in British Politics Since 1968 (Stanford, Calif.: Hoover Institution Press).

Dye, Thomas (1980). "Taxing, Spending, and Economic Growth in the American States," Journal of Politics 42 (November): 1085-1107.

Eckstein, Otto, Christopher Caton, Roger Brinner, and Peter Duprey (1984). The DRI Report on US Manufacturing Industries (New York: McGraw Hill).

Elvander, N. (1979). "Sweden," in Towards Industrial Democracy: Europe, Japan, and the United States, edited by B. Roberts (Montclair: Allanheld, OSMUN).

English, Maurice (1984). "The European Technology Industry," in European Industry: Public Policy

and Corporate Strategy, edited by Alexis
Jacquemin (Oxford: Clarendon Press).

Estrin, S., and P. Holmes (1983). "French Planning
and Industrial Policy," Journal of Public
Policy 3: 131-48.

Etzioni, A. (1983). "The MITIzation of America?"
The Public Interest 72: 44-52.

Europa-Archiv (1978) 23: D11-19.

Europäische Gemeinschaften (1967). Erstes Programm
für die mittelfristige Wirtschaftspolitik,
1966-1970 (Brussels: European Community).

Europäische Gemeinschaften (1969). Zweites Programm für die Mittlefristige Wirtschaftspolitik (Brussels: European Community).

European Commission (1977). "Communication on the
Perspectives of an Economic and Monetary
Union" (November 17).

European Community Bulletin (1973-1982) various
issues.

Eurostadt Review 1970-1979 (1981). (Luxembourg:
European Communities).

Farrands, Chris (1979). "Textile Diplomacy: The
Making and Implementation of European Textile
Policy," Journal of Common Market Studies 18:
22-39.

Fiorina, Morris P. (1977). Congress: Keystone of
the Washington Establishment (New Haven,
Conn.: Yale University Press).

Fitzgerald, R., and G. Lipson (1984). Pork Barrel
(Washington, D.C.: The Cato Institute).

Franzmeyer, Fritz (1979). Industrielle Struktur-
probleme und sektorale Strukturpolitik (Berlin: Duncker & Humblot).

Geister, Hans-Armin (1983)."Wettewerbs-und In-
dustriepolitik," in Jahrbuch der Europäischen
Integration 1982, edited by Werner Weidenfeld
and Wolfgang Wessels (Bonn: Europa Union Ver-
lag.

Gibson, James L., Cornelius P. Cotter, John F.
Bibby, and Robert J. Huckshorn (1983)."Assess-
ing Party Organizational Strength," American
Journal of Political Science 27 (May):193-222.

Götz, Christian (1984)."Regimeverhandlungen in den
Europäischen Gemtinschaften, Ph.D. Dissertation, University of Salzburg.

Gourevitch, Peter et al. (1984). Unions and Economic Crisis: Britain, West Germany and Sweden
(London: George Allen and Unwin).

Grant, Wyn (1982). The Political Economy of Industrial Policy (London: Butterworths).

Gray, J.C., and D.A. Spina (1980). "State and Local Industrial Location Incentives: A Well-Stocked Candy Store," Journal of Corporation Law 5: 517-687.

Hall, P.A. (1983). "Policy Innovation and the Structure of the State: The Politics-Administration Nexus in France and Britain," The Annals 466 (March): 43-60.

Hansen, S.B. (1984). "The Effects of State Industrial Policies on Economic Growth," Paper presented at annual meeting of the American Political Science Association, Washington, D.C.

Hardin, G. (1966). "The Tragedy of the Commons," Science 162: 1243-48.

Harwood, Richard C. (1985). Industrial Policy as a National Issue: A Bibliography (Princeton, N.J.: Princeton University Urban and Regional Research Center).

Hatsopoulos, G. (1983). High Cost of Capital: Handicap of American Industry (New York: American Business Conference).

Heclo, Hugh (1978a). A Government of Strangers (Washington, D.C.: The Brookings Institution).

Heclo, Hugh (1978b). "Issue Networks and the Executive Establishment," in The New American Political System, edited by A. King (Washington, D.C.: American Enterprise Institute).

Heisler, M.O. (1979). "Corporate Pluralism Revisited: Where is the Theory?" Scandinavian Political Studies 2: 277-97.

Hills, J. (1983). "The Industrial Policy of Japan," Journal of Public Policy 3: 63-80.

Hoffman, Stanley (1977). "The Uses of American Power," Foreign Affairs 56 (October): 27-48.

Hogwood, B.W., and B.G. Peters (1985). The Pathology of Policy (Oxford: Oxford University Press).

Hudson, W., M.S. Hyde, and J. Carroll (n.d.). "Corporatist Policymaking and State Economic Development" (Providence, R.I.: Department of Political Science, Providence College) Mimeo.

Industrial Innovation: A Guide to Community Action, Services and Funding (1983). (Brussels: Agence Europe/European Research Associates).

112

International Labor Organization (1983). _Wirt-_
    schafts-und Sozialstatistisches Taschenbuch
    (Vienna: Österreichischer Arbeiterkammertag
International Research Group (IRG) (1981). _Indus-_
    trial Democracy in Europe. International Re-
    search Group (Oxford: Clarendon Press).
Jacobs, J. (1980). _Bidding for Business: Corporate_
    Auctions and the Fifty Disunited States
    (Washington, D.C.: Public Interest Research
    Group).
Jacquemin, Alexis (1984). "Introduction: Which
    Policy for Industry," in _European Industry:_
    Public Policy and Corporate Strategy, edited
    by Alexis Jacquemin (Oxford: Clarendon Press).
Jéquier, Nicolas (1974). "Computers," in _Big_
    Business and the State, edited by Raymond
    Vernon (Cambridge, Mass.: Harvard University
    Press).
Johnson, C. (1982). _MITI and the Japanese Miracle_
    (Stanford, Calif.: Stanford University Press).
Jordan, A.G. (1981). "Iron Triangles, Woolly Cor-
    poratism, or Elastic Nets: Images of the
    Policy Process," _Journal of Public Policy_ 1:
    95-124.
Katzenstein, P.J. (1984). _Corporatism and Change:_
    Austria, Switzerland and the Politics of In-
    dustry (Ithaca, N.Y.: Cornell University
    Press).
Kendall, Walter (1975). _The Labour Movement in_
    Europe (London: Allan Lane).
King, Anthony (1976). "Ideas, Institutions and
    Policies of Governments: A Comparative An-
    alysis," _British Journal of Political Science_
    3: 301-23, 409-23.
Kingdon, John R. (1984). _Agendas, Alternatives_
    and Public Policies (Boston: Little, Brown).
Klein, Lawrence R. (1983). "Identifying the Effects
    of Structural Change," in _Industrial Change_
    and Public Policy (Kansas City, Mo.: Federal
    Reserve Bank of Kansas City).
Kommission der Europäischen Wirtschaftsgemein-
    schaft (1963). _Memorandum der Kommission_
    über das Aktionsprogramm der Gemeinschaft
    für die Zweite Stufe (Europa Archiv).
Kvavik, R. (1978). _Interest Groups in Norwegian_
    Politics (Oslo: Universitetsforlaget).

Lafferty, William L. (1984). "The Democratization of Capital: A Comparative Analysis of Alternative Social Democratic Approaches." Paper presented to the Workshop on Industrial Democracy, ECPR, Salzburg.

Lauber, Volkmar (1983a). "From Growth Consensus to Fragmentation in Western Europe," Comparative Politics 15: 329-49.

Lauber, Volkmar (1983b). Launching High-Technology Business in Europe (Brussels: Agence Europe/ European Research Associates).

Lawrence, R.Z. (1984). Can America Compete? (Washington, D.C.: Brookings Institution).

Lawrence, R.Z. (1985). "Comments on Do We Need an Industrial Policy?" Harpers (February), pp. 35-48.

Lehmbruch, Gerhard, and Philippe C. Schmitter, eds. (1982). Patterns of Corporatist Policy-Making (Beverly Hills, Calif.: Sage).

LeLoup, Lance T., and Steven A. Shull (1979). "Congress Versus the Executive: The 'Two Presidencies' Reconsidered," Social Science Quarterly 59 (March): 704-19.

Lesourne, Jacques (1985). "The Changing Context of Industrial Policy: External and Internal Developments," in European Industry: Public Policy and Corporate Strategy, edited by Alexis Jacquemin (Oxford: Clarendon Press).

Levinson, Charles, ed. (1974). Industry's Democratic Revolution (London: George Allen and Unwin.

Lindbeck, A. (1976). Swedish Economic Policy (Berkeley, Calif.: University of California Press).

Lowi, Theodore J. (1964). "American Business, Public Policy, Case Studies, and Political Theory," World Politics 16 (July): 677-715.

Lowi, Theodore J. (1972). "Four Systems of Policy, Politics, and Choice," Public Administration Review 32 (July-August): 298-310.

McKay, D. (1983). "Industrial Policy and Non-policy in the United States," Journal of Public Policy 3: 29-48.

McKay, D., and W. Grant (1983). "Industrial Policies in OECD Countries," Journal of Public Policy 3: 1-12.

114

Mayhew, David (1974). Congress: The Electoral Connection (New Haven, Conn.: Yale University Press).

Mielke, Siegfried, ed. (1983). Internationales Gewerkschaftshandbuch (Opladen: Leske and Budrich).

Mosher, Frederick C. (1980). "The Changing Responsibilities and Tactics of the Federal Government," Public Administration Review 40: 541-48.

Murrell, Peter (1983). "The Comparative Structure of the Growth of the West German and British Manufacturing Industries," in The Political Economy of Growth, edited by D. Mueller (New Haven, Conn.: Yale University Press).

National Journal (1984), September 29, p. 1829.

Nelson, R.R., and R.N. Langlois (1983). "Industrial Innovation Policy: Lessons from American History," Science (February 18), pp. 814-18.

Nice, David (1984). "Interest Groups and Policymaking in the American States," Political Behavior 6: 183-96.

Olson, David (1985). "Reagan and Congress: Economic and Industrial Policy." Paper presented at the annual meeting of the American Political Science Association, New Orleans, La., August 29-September 1.

Olson, Mancur (1965). The Logic of Collective Action (Cambridge, Mass.: Harvard University Press).

Olson, Mancur (1982). The Rise and Decline of Nations: Economic Growth, Stagflation, and Social Rigidities (New Haven, Conn.: Yale University Press).

Olson, Mancur (1983). "The Political Economy of Comparative Growth Rates," in The Political Economy of Growth, edited by Dennis Mueller (New Haven, Conn.: Yale University Press).

Organski, A.F.K., and Jacek Kugler (1977). "The Costs of Major Wars: The Phoenix Factor," American Political Science Review 71 (December): 1347-66.

Pelinka, Anton (1980). Gewerkschaften im Parteiensta t: Ein Vergleich Zwischen dem Deutschen und dem Österreichischen Gewerkschaftsbund (Berlin: Duncker and Humblot).

Pelinka, Anton (1981). Modellfall Österreich? Möglichkeiten und Grenzen der Sozial Partnerschaft (Vienna: Braümuller).

Pelinka, Anton (1983). Social Democratic Parties in Europe (New York: Praeger).

Peters, B. Guy (1981). "The Problem of Party Government," Journal of Politics 43: 56-82.

Peters, B. Guy (1984a). "Economic Development in Louisiana," in Insights (New Orleans, La.: Center for Public Policy Studies, Tulane University).

Peters, B. Guy (1984b). The Politics of Bureaucracy, 2nd ed. (New York: Longman).

Peters, B. Guy (1985). "The Grace Commission and Public Management," in The Unfinished Agenda of Civil Service Reform, edited by Charles H. Levine (Washington, D.C.: The Brookings Institution).

Phillips, Kevin P. (1984). "We Need to Adopt a Conservative Industrial Strategy," Washington Post National Weekly Edition (December 31), pp. 22-23.

Polsby, Nelson (1984). Political Innovations in America (New Haven, Conn.: Yale University Press).

Presidential Commission on Industrial Competitiveness (1985). Global Competition: The New Reality (Washington, D.C.: Government Printing Office).

Pressman, Jeffrey, and Aaron Wildavsky (1984). Implementation, 3rd ed. (Berkeley, Calif.: University of California Press).

Pryor, Frederic L. (1983). "A Quasi-test of Olson's Hypotheses," in The Political Economy of Growth, edited by D. Mueller (New Haven, Conn.: Yale University Press).

Ranney, Austin (1971). "Parties in State Politics," in Politics in the American States: A Comparative Analysis, edited by Herbert Jacob and Kenneth Vines, 2nd ed. (Boston: Little, Brown).

Ranney, Austin, and Wilmore Kendall (1956). Democracy and the American Party System (New York: Harcourt, Brace).

Ray, James Lee (1984). "Book Review of Olson's Rise and Decline," Journal of Politics 46 (August): 985-87.

Redwood, J. (1984). Going for Broke: Gambling with
    the Taxpayers' Money (Oxford: Basil Blackwell).
Reich, Robert B. (1983). The Next American Frontier
    (New York: Times Books).
Reich, Robert B. and I. Magaziner (1982). Minding
    America's Business: The Decline and Rise of
    the American Economy (New York: Harcourt,
    Brace, Jovanovich).
Roberts, Benjamin C. (1979a). "United Kingdom," in
    Toward Industrial Democracy: Europe, Japan,
    and the United States, edited by B. Roberts
    (Montclair: Allenheld, Osmun).
Roberts, Benjamin C., ed. (1979b). Toward Indus-
    trial Democracy: Europe, Japan, and the United
    States (Montclair: Allenheld, Osmun).
Rohatyn, Felix (1983). The Twenty-Year Century
    (New York: Random House).
Rohatyn, Felix (1984). "American Roulette," New
    York Review, March 29, pp. 11-15.
Rose, Richard (1974). The Problem of Party Govern-
    ment (London: Macmillan).
Rose, Richard (1975). Managing Presidential Objec-
    tives (New York: Macmillan).
Rose, Richard (1984). Do Parties Make a Difference?
    (Chatham, N.J.: Chatham House).
Salisbury, Robert H. (1979). "Why No Corporatism
    in America?" in Trends Toward Corporatist
    Intermediation, edited by P.C. Schmitter and
    G. Lehmbruch (Beverly Hills, Calif.: Sage).
Schattschneider, E.E. (1960). The Semi-Sovereign
    People (New York: Holt, Rinehart, and Winston).
Schlesinger, Joseph (1966). Ambition and Politics:
    Political Careers in the United States (Chi-
    cago: Rand McNally).
Schmitter, Philippe C. (1974). "Still the Century
    of Corporatism?" Review of Politics 36: 85-
    131.
Schmitter, Philippe C. (1979). "Modes of Interest
    Intermediation and Models of Societal Change
    in Western Europe," in Trends Towards Corpor-
    atist Intermediation, edited by P. Schmitter
    and G. Lehmbruch (Beverly Hills, Calif.: Sage).
Schmitter, Philippe C. and Gerhard Lehmbruch, eds.
    (1979). Trends Towards Corporatist Intermedi-
    ation (Beverly Hills, Calif.: Sage).
Schulman, Paul R. (1980). Large-Scale Policy Mak-
    ing (New York: Elsevier).

Schultze, Charles (1983). "Industrial Policy: A Dissent," Brookings Review, Fall, pp. 3-13.

Schwartz, J.E. (1983). America's Hidden Success (New York: Norton).

Sharkansky, Ira (1978). Wither the State? (Chatham, N.J.: Chatham House).

Shepherd, Geoffrey (1984). "Industrial Change in European Countries: The Experience of Six Sectors," in European Industry: Public Policy and Corporate Strategy (Oxford: Clarendon Press).

Shonfield, Andrew (1969). Modern Capitalism (Oxford: Oxford University Press).

Shull, Steven A. (1983). Domestic Policy Formation: Presidential-Congressional Partnership? (Westport, Conn.: Greenwood Press).

Sidenius, N.C. (1983). "Danish Industrial Policy: Persistent Liberalism," Journal of Public Policy 3: 49-62.

Stein, Herbert (1983). "U.S. Foreign Trade and Trade Policy," AEI Economist, July, p. 3.

Steinbach, C., and Niel R. Pierce (1984). "Cities are Setting their Sights on International Trade and Investment," National Journal, April 28, pp. 818-22.

Sundquist, James L. (1978). "A Comparison of the Policy-Making Capacity in the United States and Five European Countries: The Case of Population Distribution," in Population Policy Analyses, edited by Michael E. Kraft and Mark Schneider. (Lexington, Mass.: D.C. Heath).

Thayer, Frederick (1984). Rebuilding America (New York: Praeger).

Thorn, Gaston (1984). Berichte und Informationen (Bonn: Press and Information Office, European Community), February 23.

U.S. House of Representatives (1977). Oversight of the Anti-Dumping Act of 1921, Subcommittee on Trade, Committee on Ways and Means, 95th Congress, 1st Session (Washington, D.C.: Government Printing Office).

U.S. House of Representatives (1978). Administration's Comprehensive Program for the Steel Industry. Subcommittee on Trade, Committee on Ways and Means, 95th Congress, 2nd Session (Washington, D.C.: Government Printing Office).

U.S. House of Representatives (1984). Industrial
    Competitiveness Act, Committee on Banking,
    Finance and Urban Affairs, 98th Congress,
    2nd Session (Washington, D.C.: Government
    Printing Office).
Vernon, Raymond (1974). "Enterprise and Government
    in Western Europe," in Big Business and the
    State, edited by Raymond Vernon (Cambridge,
    Mass.: Harvard University Press).
Von Beyme, Klaus (1980). Challenge to Power, Trade
    Unions and Industrial Relations in Capitalist
    Countries (London: Sage).
Walker, Jack (1969). "The Diffusion of Innovations
    Among the American States," American Politi-
    cal Science Review 63 (September): 880-99.
Walters, R.S. (1984). "Strategic Economic and In-
    dustrial Vulnerability: Challenges to Policy
    and Analysis in the United States." Paper
    prepared for the Institute for Strategic Eco-
    nomics and Industrial Vulnerability, Univer-
    sity of Pittsburgh, Pittsburgh, Pa.
Weidenbaum, Murray (1983). "Toward a More Open
    Trade Policy." St. Louis: Washington Univer-
    sity Center for the Study of American Busi-
    ness, Vol. 53, January, pp. 34-35.
Wells, Louis T. (1984). "Automobiles," in Big
    Business and the State, edited by Raymond
    Vernon (Cambridge, Mass.: Harvard University
    Press).
Wildavsky, Aaron (1966). "Two Presidencies," Trans-
    Action 4 (December): 7-14.
Wilkinson, Christopher (1984). "Trends in Industri-
    al Policy in the EC: Theory and Practice," in
    European Industry: Public Policy and Corporate
    Strategy, edited by Alexis Jacquemin (Oxford:
    Clarendon Press).
Wilson, James Q. (1980). The Politics of Regula-
    tion (New York: Basic Books).
Zeigler, L. Harmon, and Hendrik van Dalen (1971).
    "Interest Groups in the States," in Politics
    in the American States: A Comparative Analy-
    sis, edited by Herbert Jacob and Kenneth
    Vines, 2nd ed. (Boston: Little, Brown).
Zysman, J. (1983). Governments, Markets and
    Growth: Financial Systems and the Politics
    of Industrial Change (Ithaca, N.Y.: Cornell
    University Press).

Contributors

GREGORY G. BRUNK, Assistant Professor of Political Science at the University of Oklahoma, received his Ph.D. from the University of Iowa in 1981. His major research interests are American government and political economy. He has published in numerous journals, including <u>American Journal of Political Science</u> and <u>Public Choice</u>.

JEFFREY E. COHEN, Associate Professor of Political Science at the University of New Orleans, received his Ph.D. in Political Science from the University of Michigan in 1979. His major research interests include American government and regulatory policy. He has published in numerous journals, including the <u>American Political Science Review</u>.

WERNER J. FELD, Distinguished Professor of Political Science at the University of New Orleans, and Director of the Institute for the Comparative Study of Public Policy, is the author of many books and articles. His latest book is <u>Congress and National Defense</u>. Professor Feld specializes in American foreign policy, international relations (both governmental and nongovernmental) and the politics of Western Europe.

VOLKMAR LAUBER, Professor of Political Science at the University of Salzburg, has a major interest in comparative political economy. His latest book is entitled <u>The Politics of Economic Policy: France, 1976-82</u>. He is Vice

President of the Austrian Political Science
Association.
ROBERT LAWRENCE, an Economist with the Brookings
Institution, received his Ph.D. from Yale
University. His major research interests
include economics and international trade,
and among his latest publications is Can
America Compete?
ANTON PELINKA, Professor and Director, Institute
of Political Science, University of Innsbruck, received his Ph.D. from the University of Salzburg. His major research interests are political theory and comparative
politics. Author of many books, his Social
Democratic Parties in Europe has recently
been published. He is President of the
Austrian Political Science Association.
B. GUY PETERS, is the Maurice Falk Professor of
American Politics at the University of Pitts-
burgh. His major research interests are in
comparative public policy and political economy. His book, The Politics of Bureaucracy:
A Comparative Perspective, was recently re-
issued in a second edition. He is editor of
Policy Studies Journal.
STEVEN A. SHULL, Professor of Political Science,
University of New Orleans, received his Ph.D.
from Ohio State University. His major areas
of interest are the presidency and public
policy. Author and co-editor of numerous
volumes, his latest book is Domestic Policy
Formation: Presidential-Congressional Partnership?